THE ROAD TO UTOPIA

THE ROAD TO UTOPIA

How Kinky, Tony, & I Saved More Animals Than Noah

NANCY PARKER-SIMONS

Foreword by Kinky Friedman

University of Texas Press
Austin

Requests for permission to reproduce material from this work should be sent to:
    Permissions
    University of Texas Press
    P.O. Box 7819
    Austin, TX 78713-7819
    www.utexas.edu/utpress/about/bpermission.html

∞ The paper used in this book meets the minimum requirements of ANSI/NISO z39.48-1992 (R1997) (Permanence of Paper).

Library of Congress Cataloging-in-Publication Data

Parker-Simons, Nancy, 1951–
    The road to Utopia : how Kinky, Tony, and I saved more animals than Noah / by Nancy Parker-Simons ; foreword by Kinky Friedman. — 1st ed.
        p.   cm.
    ISBN-13: 978-0-292-71408-3 ((cl.) : alk. paper)
    ISBN-10: 0-292-71408-4
    ISBN-13: 978-0-292-71488-5 ((pbk.) : alk. paper)
    ISBN-10: 0-292-71488-2
    1. Dogs—Texas—Anecdotes. 2. Animal rescue—Texas—Anecdotes. 3. Utopia Animal Rescue Ranch (Tex.). 4. Parker-Simons, Nancy, 1951–   I. Title.
    SF426.2.P37 2006
    636.08'32—dc22

                                                                    2006006555

Portions of this work have appeared in a different form on the Utopia Animal Rescue Ranch website: www.utopiarescue.com

"Epilogue for Cuddles" is reprinted with permission from the author.
Photo on p. x by Jill Johnson, courtesy of the *Fort Worth Star-Telegram*

In Texas, *it is often said that you gotta dance with the one who brung you. I totally agree with that, and I wish to thank Kinky Friedman, Tony Simons, and Ben Welch for dancing with me. I love y'all!*

IN DOG WE TRUST

Contents

PART SEVEN
Keepin' on the Sunny Side

Foreword

Cousin Nancy isn't really my cousin; she's much more than that. She not only looks after me, as well as her husband, Tony, and more animals than Noah could ever have shoehorned onto the Ark, but she's also the main reason, I believe, that Utopia Animal Rescue Ranch has survived and thrived for eight years and counting. Her secret, as far as I can tell, is a special combination of love, dedication, and a really wicked sense of humor, the last being an absolute necessity for anyone who runs an orphanage, a halfway house, or a hospice of the two-legged or the four-legged variety.

Nancy has seen the best and the worst that people can do. She has witnessed many of the lessons animals—especially stray and abused animals—can teach us about some of the most important things in life: how to love, how to be loyal, how to learn how to trust, how to learn to forgive, how to live every moment, how to always be ready for fun. For their part, Nancy and Tony teach the animals that people can be good.

Cousin Nancy is a very funny woman. I've read her hilarious Rescue Ranch newsletters over the years, but I wasn't prepared for what happened when I started to read these wonderful stories of Utopia. A voice was speaking to me, the reader, in a way I had never heard before. The experience was uniquely evocative of the simple, down-home, truth-telling style of a Will Rogers, or a Ring Lardner, or a Mark Twain. Furry characters seemed to be leaping off the pages into my consciousness and into my heart. When I finished the book, one eye was laughing and one eye was crying.

The Road to Utopia is the chronicle of the many dogs who've found loving homes, the many who left Utopia with their new people, still looking wistfully over their shoulders at the only happy home they'd ever known, and the tragic few who crossed the rainbow bridge without ever being adopted. According to Cousin Nancy, all of them, in one way or another, will live forever in Utopia. Their stories are here, told in a way that every child (and most adults) can understand if they only remember to read between the lines.

For in the final analysis, this is not just a book about animals. Like *Charlotte's Web* or the movie *Babe*, it may subtly change the way we look at the world, or, perhaps more significantly, the way we see ourselves. Taking care of the homeless, the forgotten, the outcasts, the ones who have lost their way, a basic tenet of Christianity and America itself, is something that goes on every day at Utopia, if not always in the world outside. Cousin Nancy's book may, indeed, be that timely beacon that, once again, reminds us all what a little love can do.

KINKY FRIEDMAN
Medina, Texas
January 1, 2006

A Note from the Author

You would not be reading this book had fate not played its hand on Saturday, April 30, 2005, when I reluctantly answered the rescue ranch telephone at 3:42 p.m. Usually, I always let the machine screen the calls, but for some reason I decided to pick up the phone.

"Hello, Nancy? This is Sandy at Wolfmueller's Books in Kerrville."

"Well, hi, Sandy. How are you?" I asked.

"Fine. Look, the reason that I'm calling is that there are two women here from Austin who would love to come out and see the rescue ranch. Is it too late?"

I looked at the clock on the kitchen wall—it was eighteen minutes before the rescue ranch would be officially closed for the day and I was feeling tired.

"No," I said, "it's not too late. Tell them to come on out."

Thirty minutes later, two women showed up at the ranch and were eager to take a tour. Tony was busy feeding the dogs, so I showed them around. After the tour I invited them into my writing studio, which also now serves as a halfway house for our elderly dogs to enjoy.

As everyone knows, Libras like to talk a lot, and since I am a full-blown Libra, I went on a gabbing spree about being a writer that nobody had ever heard of—because I hadn't been published, yet—blah, blah, blah.

"This is incredible!" Allison said, when she finally got a word in edgewise. "Sheri and I both work in books. I am with the University of Texas Press; we publish on a variety of subjects, but we don't do fiction."

We visited a little while longer. As they were about to leave, Allison handed me her business card. We said our goodbyes; they drove away and

I went back inside the trailer. Ten minutes hadn't passed when I picked up the phone and dialed Allison's business number.

"Allison, this is Nancy and y'all just left here, but I was just thinking that I needed to tell you that I am planning on writing a book about the story of the Utopia Animal Rescue Ranch," I said to her answering machine. "I don't know . . . something just told me to give you a call and let you know. Bye."

Monday morning, at nine o'clock, Allison called me. She told me that she and Sheri had talked the entire drive back up to Austin about me writing a book about the rescue ranch! She then asked me if I could get a book proposal to her before Wednesday, the day that the Press was meeting to discuss book proposals.

Friday afternoon, I received my contract to write this book.

I feel so very honored to tell the story of the Utopia Animal Rescue Ranch. Even though the rescue ranch recently celebrated its eight-year anniversary, it still seems just like yesterday when Kinky Friedman drove out to my small ranch in Utopia, Texas, and proposed his idea to my soon-to-be future husband, Tony Simons, and me about the three of us creating a sanctuary for abandoned animals.

To date we have rescued more than a thousand animals, and having to decide which stories to tell was not easy for me to do. Some are sad or depressing or maddening or funny or just plain incredibly beautiful. Being a Libra, I primarily chose the happy stories to tell, but I did include some others that touched Kinky's, Tony's, and my heart and needed to be told. Also, please note that in a few of the stories the names of the animals or people had to be changed.

Living every day at the rescue ranch, with at least sixty dogs, a dozen chickens, eight precious pigs, a proud rooster that only crows at the crack of noon, twenty horses, two wild mustangs (which caused me to have an unwanted near-death experience—a ride-by), several cats, twenty or so wild Russian boars, two donkeys—including a miniature one—raccoons, porcupines, rattlesnakes, deer, scorpions, lizards, turtles, millions of hummingbirds and butterflies, and an occasional mountain lion is exciting to say the least!

Every morning I start out with a list of things to do, and usually by ten o'clock everything changes. On the average, our ranch receives no less than twenty phone calls a day from people desperately wanting us to take their animals, but we can't because we stay full, and we refuse to warehouse our dogs. Our policy is when a dog gets adopted, we go to the pound to replace it.

Tony's and my job is twenty-four/seven. We are open to the public on Saturdays, but people show up out here every day, either hoping to meet Kinky, or to dump or adopt an animal or take a tour. We are closed on Sundays and all holidays, but Tony and I cannot leave the ranch, because that's when people driving around in the Hill Country want to visit the rescue ranch. It may sound as if I'm whining, but I'm not—we enjoy meeting people and we have grown accustomed to this kind of lifestyle—and we love being with the animals.

Kinky often teases us about "not getting out much," or not taking enough vacations, but he is preaching to deaf ears, because living here at Echo Hill is a blast! If we aren't busy taking care of the animals, or rescuing, or cooking quesadillas for the dogs, or running back and forth to Kerrville, or taking care of office business—we have Kinky to entertain us. When he is around, there is no telling what will happen out here. He has introduced us to some of the most interesting people, including many celebrities.

When Kinky is home at Echo Hill Ranch, the three of us usually share meals while discussing the goings-on at the rescue ranch. Every visitor who comes out to see Kinky winds up taking a tour of the rescue ranch and is asked by Kinky to adopt one or two of our dogs. He is like a used car salesman when it comes to adopting one of our dogs, and he can be extremely persistent—just ask his friends.

With Tony and me being full-time employees, our rescue ranch has five part-time employees—Maribeth Couch, Ben Welch, Jack Anglin, De'Andrey Wingwood, and Daniel Hudson—who have been invaluable to us with their fine skills and hard work. We also are lucky enough to have nine of the greatest and most dedicated and caring volunteers in the whole state of Texas: June Hartley, Ellen Jackson, Paul and Marty Emerson, Will Wallace, Ellen and Charlie Cooper, Sally Merwyn, and Max Swafford. We love every one of our helpers and so do our dogs!

So, now that I have told you about what our daily life is like at the rescue ranch, I invite you to come out and adopt one or two of our dogs. And, if you are lucky, Kinky might just be around.

Louise, our Grand Dame

June with Albert & Macy

Team Utopia

PART ONE

The Road to Utopia

Be my valentine

Will bark for food

Maribeth and Sally

Taking a break:
De'Andrey, Ben, & Daniel

Nelda with Little Jewford

Fated Love

The first dog that I ever knew was our family dog, Tuffy. He was a sweet, medium-sized mutt who loved me, and who also taught me how to walk by letting me hold on to his crooked tail.

By the ripe old age of fourteen, in the early 60s, I thought I was the richest girl in Fort Worth, Texas, because my first real paying job was taking care of the baby animals at the Fort Worth Zoo's Children's Petting Zoo.

My job was a dream come true for me, because I loved animals and was being paid one dollar an hour to clean up, feed, and look after all kinds of baby animals. For over three years, I spent every weekend during the school year, and five days a week during the summer months, working at the Children's Zoo.

I hand-raised fawns, lambs, monkeys, rabbits, wallabies, donkeys, goats, sheep, turtles, birds of all kinds, ducks, piglets, and a baby elephant. And being given the authority to name each and every one of these animals was icing on the cake for me. Most of the time, I would name an animal after my current boyfriend, so there were often many name changes, but the animals did not seem to care. One of the neatest things that happened to me at the zoo was when I got to hold and bottle-feed a baby orangutan that was less than three days old!

After my zoo years, I worked for veterinarians, went to college, and then got married, divorced, and then went back to working for veterinarians in Fort Worth—until I got married for the second time.

My new husband, Jim Parker, was in the oil and gas business, and soon after we married he asked me to start a business that could be used as a tax write-off—in other words, he needed losses. I told him that I wanted to do doggie day care or something like that, but he suggested that I think of some other kind of business that wouldn't take up too much of my time. He wanted me married to him, not to the dogs.

So I started a one-day turnaround embroidery business in Fort

Worth. My business ended up going through the roof, while his bit the dust in 1986. After that wonderful experience, I sold my business in Fort Worth, and we moved to Austin, where we teamed up and started a new embroidery business in Westlake, Texas.

We took our four dogs—Yoda, a Boston Terrier, Chili, a Sheltie, Chaser, a big, red mutt, and Bear, a Great Pyrenees—to work with us every day. We were in one of the wealthiest neighborhoods in Austin, and our dogs soon became celebrities to our customers' kids. Our customers would bring garments in to be embroidered just so their kids could come to play with our dogs.

Our dogs were an asset to our business—except for one disastrous occasion. Chaser took off one afternoon and didn't return to our shop for over an hour. When she finally returned she was bloated to twice her normal size. A few minutes later, we discovered what had happened to her. The owner of the barbecue place next door to us had caught Chaser stealing a brisket off of his pit and running away with it.

We apologized, paid him for the brisket, and then we had to pay dearly the rest of the afternoon—smelling her foul farts. Near closing time that day, a wealthy customer came into our shop. He and I were shooting the bull and discussing his embroidery job when the worst odor that I have ever smelled descended upon us. It was as if a sewer line had busted. I didn't want him thinking the smell was from me, so I quickly fanned my nose and apologized to him, and told him that the horrible smell was from my dog who had just eaten an entire brisket. He just stood there smiling at me. I pointed down to where my dog usually lies by the counter, but she wasn't there. I then turned around and saw Jim walking all four of our dogs outside. It took a second for me to realize that it was the customer who had farted, and I rapidly turned about eight shades of red. It was extremely embarrassing for me.

In 1990, our friend and the number one deejay in Austin, Sammy Allred, came to our shop to introduce us to his friend Kinky Friedman. Kinky came because he wanted to order a couple of our Geezinslaw Brothers Shiny Nineties Tour jackets for himself and his sister, Marcie. Having heard numerous rave reviews from Sammy over the past years about how funny Kinky's books were, I cut a deal with Kinky for the jackets. I promised him two custom-made jackets in exchange for signed first editions of his first three books. We shook hands on it, and we had us a deal.

I sewed the jackets and mailed them off to him at Echo Hill Ranch. One week later, Jim and I received all three first editions of Kinky's first three books signed to us, using our monikers that Sammy Allred had bestowed on us—Cousin Jimmy and Cousin Nancy.

Kinky's and our paths crossed several more times in the following years, usually backstage at the Austin Aqua Festival or at one of Willie's Fourth of July picnics. Jim and I fell in love with Kinky's books and always looked forward to his next one. When I read Kinky's "Epilogue to Cuddles," his late cat, in his book *Elvis, Jesus & Coca-Cola*, I cried. Up to that point, I had been clueless as to what kind of a man Kinky Friedman really was until he literally let the cat out of the bag with that epilogue. It showed me and his readership that Kinky was a kind, sensitive, loving man with a heart as big as Alaska!

By 1994, our shop, thanks to Sammy Allred, was about as successful as it could be. We were doing jobs for the who's who of the Austin music scene. Our customers included Jerry Jeff Walker, Ray Benson, Asleep at the Wheel, the Bellamy Brothers, Joe Ely, the Geezinslaw Brothers, Haywire, Eric Johnson, and PBS's *Austin City Limits*!

When Kinky's book *Armadillo and Old Lace* came out that fall, Jim and I decided after reading it to put our shop up for sale and move to the Texas Hill Country—Utopia to be exact.

In late December 1994, Jim became ill with the flu—we thought. As the weeks went by, Jim's condition got worse instead of better. Even though we did have good insurance, we didn't have a lot of faith in the medical industry; we avoided doctors like the plague, until Jim had gotten in such a bad way that we decided that he needed medical care. My brother-in-law, Ray Roche, volunteered to take Jim to the hospital to get him checked out so that I could keep our shop open. At the end of the day, I closed the shop and, with my four dogs, drove over to the hospital to pick Jim up.

When I arrived at the hospital, I found Jim in a bed in the emergency room with tubes running out of his arms—and he looked scared. Before I could reach him, a young doctor met up with me and told me that he was a brain surgeon; he then said that Jim was eaten up with cancer and needed immediate brain surgery to remove the tumors, or else he would die within a matter of days.

I felt like I had just been hit in the head by Babe Ruth swinging a giant baseball bat.

The following day Jim had his brain surgery, and fortunately it was successful—sort of. The doctors gave him thirty to forty days to live at most. A week later, Jim came home.

He passed away peaceably at home thirty-five days later, with me and the dogs at his bedside. And, the following week, my Great Pyrenees, Bear, had to be euthanized.

Knowing full well that I couldn't run the shop without Jim, I decided to put it on the market. Two days later it sold.

Looking back now, I realize that I would have never survived my loss if it wasn't for the love from my dogs. They helped to fill the void that Jim left. After about a month of crying myself to sleep and wearing only black sweat suits, I grew tired of the role of the grieving widow. Jim was dead and he wasn't coming back, and I was tired of being depressed. It was time to get on with my life and move on.

The first thing I did to get things rolling again was to have a little talk with God about Him possibly helping me find a little ranch that was affordable in Utopia, Texas. Even though He never spoke to me, He must have heard me, because one week later one of my dreams came true. I became the proud owner of a beautiful mini-ranch in Utopia, Texas! It was all so easy: I bought the first ranch that the realtor showed me because it gave me a special feeling in my heart. I knew I was meant to buy it—it had been waiting for me.

My ranch, which I immediately named Rolling Thunder after a dead medicine man, was perfect. It was ten giant acres, completely fenced, with a huge stock tank, an old goat barn, cedar and oak trees galore, and, to top it off, it had one of the prettiest views of the mountains. I was in Utopia! Next came the water, electricity, septic tank, and the 1983 used trailer, which was in excellent shape and affordable, that I bought from Bob and Helen Wightman in Utopia. The dogs and I then happily moved to Utopia on August 1, 1995. I am still amazed at how everything had just seemed to fall into place so easily for me. I remember feeling that I was meant to come to Utopia for a reason, but I didn't have a clue as to why.

By the middle of February, I was nearly broke. No one living in the country needed embroidery or could afford it. I decided to go to Kerrville, which was some sixty miles away, to knock on some doors to try to drum up some business. Little did I know that as my dogs Yoda and Chili and I drove to Kerrville that fate was fixin' to bring me face to face with my destiny.

Forty miles and forty minutes later, as we were driving down Highway 16, I passed the Echo Hill Ranch road sign. A second passed before I slammed on my brakes and pulled off the road. Something inside me told me to turn around and go see Kinky Friedman at his family ranch, Echo Hill. So I did.

Upon entering the ranch, I met Kinky's sister, Marcie, who was on her way out of the ranch. She drove up to me and asked me if I needed help. I told her that I was looking for Kinky. She told me that she was meeting him for lunch in Kerrville and asked me if I wanted to follow her to the restaurant to see him. My answer was yes, but I didn't exactly follow her—it was more like flying, because Marcie drove faster than the speed of sound!

When we reached the restaurant, my stomach was upset, because I had never driven that fast in my entire lifetime. Marcie and I went inside and found Kinky. He first told me that he was sorry to hear about Jim's passing, and then asked me where I was living.

"Utopia," I answered.

Kinky smiled, not knowing that there really was a town named Utopia. Then he asked me to join them for lunch, but I declined the invitation since I had my dogs with me and was feeling nauseous. I handed him a business card and told him that I was trying to drum up some embroidery business. He took my card and told me that he would get back to me. We shook hands, and I left.

When I arrived back at my ranch, Kinky had already called my answering machine and had left a message for me to call him. I made the call immediately. He answered his phone, and our conversation was fairly short. He asked me to come over to Echo Hill to discuss some jean jackets that I might like to sew for him. Might like—might love was more like it.

I drove over to Echo Hill Ranch with my two little dogs. Kinky came out to greet me as I was getting out of my truck, and when he saw Chili and Yoda he asked me to please let them out so they could play with his young rescued dog, Mr. Magoo.

As Mr. Magoo ran, chased, and played outside with my dogs, Kinky and I talked business inside the Lodge. An hour later, I drove home with a big check and a giant jean jacket order from Kinky. He had rescued me! But little did I know that this would not be the last time that Kinky would be there for me.

The following week, after paying all of my bills, I sewed Kinky's "God Bless John Wayne" jean jackets. When I delivered the jackets to him he had two questions for me.

One, would I like to start the very first Kinky fan club for him, and run it out of my trailer in Utopia? And two, did I want to become Mr. Magoo's official babysitter? Of course, my answer to both of his questions was—yes!

Within a month, the Kinky Friedman Crime Club, financed by Kinky, was up and running on the Internet. My phone was ringing off the hook, night and day, with calls from Kinky fans who either wanted to just visit or buy merchandise.

I sold sweatshirts, hats, mugs, and posters, but unfortunately my eight-hundred-dollar-a-month phone bills were killing the profits. Kinky kept the fan club afloat for over a year, and then we shut it down. It was a lot of fun and hard work, but as he and I both agreed later on—it was not a financial pleasure for either of us.

During that same year, I met Tony Simons and fell madly in love with him at first sight. Being a Libra, my favorite saying is "it is so nice to have a man around the house (trailer)," so I invited Tony to move in with me after an extremely brief courtship. The only baggage that Tony came with was his tools, his clothes, and a cute little dog that he had rescued named Little Girl. They both fit right in, but Little Girl's name should have been Little Mama because she wound up surprising us with five adorable puppies a month later. Tony and I kept one of her sons, Hank, Sr., and found homes for the remaining four puppies.

Tony made his living by making cedar ranch furniture at my ranch, and I helped him sell it when I was not busy embroidering or babysitting Mr. Magoo.

A couple of months after Hank, Sr., was born, a friend from Utopia called to ask me if I could rescue a dog that had been dumped in downtown Utopia. She had found it eating out of trash cans and told me that the town jerk was fixin' to shoot it if I didn't come and get it. I drove to town in the rain and picked up the big, black dog and brought her home. She was a sweet, young black Labrador about six months old. Because of the stormy weather, we named her Thunder. Tony and I were now up to five dogs in the trailer—and six when Mr. Magoo vacationed with us.

On the average, Kinky was on the road two weeks out of every month, but somehow on his time off he managed to rescue animals, which, in turn, we ended up taking care of. It became an ongoing joke between the three of us. He would call and say something like, "Do y'all need another dog? I just rescued this one and . . ." And, of course, our answer was always yes.

By the time that Tony and I had accumulated a three-legged cat and ten dogs who lived with us inside our trailer, Kinky phoned to ask if we would have a meeting with him about an idea that he had. And, of course, our answer was—yes.

Let's Make a Deal

On May 23, 1998, Kinky came to our ranch in Utopia with his friend Erin and Mr. Magoo to have a picnic with us, and to discuss his idea. As the four of us sat outside on the picnic table enjoying some fried chicken and watching our dogs splashing and swimming in the stock tank, Kinky told us his idea. And it was brilliant.

After acknowledging the fact that Tony and I were up to our ears with rescued animals, which, he admitted, he had primarily planted in our laps, he proposed that the three of us start up a real rescue ranch, since we had already been rescuing dogs and cats for years.

Before we could answer, Kinky said, "Let's call it the Utopia Animal Rescue Ranch! Nancy, you have business skills, so you can do the business end. Tony can be the ranch manager, and I will be the Gandhi-like figure who will keep it afloat!" Tony and I loved Kinky's idea, and the Utopia Animal Rescue Ranch was born on that day!

Kinky wrote the following seed letter, which was sent to everyone on Echo Hill Ranch Camp's and the fan club's mailing lists. And everyone attending the Kerrville Folk Festival, at Quiet Valley Ranch, in Kerrville, found this letter in their welcome pack, thanks to friends Rod Kennedy and Dalis Allen. Here is what Kinky wrote:

Dear Friends,

Like Mark Twain and Winston Churchill, the more I see of life the less I appreciate people and the more I appreciate animals. That is why I'm writing you regarding the Animal Rescue Ranch in Utopia, Texas.

The ranch is a non-profit organization run by my friends Nancy Parker and Tony Simons who dream of eventually taking in and caring for every stray, abused, homeless, or aging animal on the planet. This is a new venture for Nancy and Tony but not a new love. They currently live with nine dogs, a small flock of sheep, a three-legged cat named Lucky, and a duck named Kathy. I will spare you the names of the dogs but horses, mules, llamas, etc., are also in their future plans. All the animals now with Nancy and Tony live together in a state of harmony almost unknown to the peoples of this world.

I've often said "Money may buy you a fine dog, but only love can make it wag its tail." Well, we have the love. Now all we need is the money. That's where we hope you'll come in.

The need for such a dream, and such a place, was made patently clear to me recently. The statistics for Kerr County alone, which are probably fairly representative of most other counties, show that last year more stray dogs and cats were destroyed, or "put down" as we say, than there are people in the county. There are well over twenty thousand people living in the Kerrville area. These animals, of course, are no longer living. There was no Rescue Ranch for them. If Nancy and Tony can help alter this truly sorry situation, I'm with them.

We'll be in touch with you as things progress and you can always call or visit us. This is one case, where, believe me, everything will come back to you ten-fold. Thanks in advance for any help you can give us. May the God who created all creatures great and small bless you.

Kinky Friedman

By September 4, 1998, along with the help of John McCall, who paid for the pens to be built, and many, many great friends and supporters, we opened the doors of our rescue ranch and rescued forty-one dogs on death row, in just three days. We were in business!

As I look back, fate played such an enormous role in putting Kinky, Tony, and me together. What if Sammy Allred had never introduced us to Kinky; what if Jim hadn't died; what if I had not been able to sell my shop; what if I hadn't moved to Utopia; what if Tony hadn't called me to go dancing; what if I had missed catching Marcie at Echo Hill that day; what if the fan club had been financially successful, etc.—then the Utopia Animal Rescue Ranch, more than likely, would have never come to be.

I will always be grateful to Sammy Allred for introducing me to Kinky Friedman—who wound up rescuing me and over a thousand animals!

The Magnificent Seven

The week before Labor Day Weekend 1998, Kinky, Tony, Marcie, and I anxiously planned our very first rescue from the Kerrville and Hondo pounds. The only critical thing that we forgot in our planning was to notify Dr. Bill Hoegemeyer at Hoegemeyer Animal Clinic in Kerrville, Texas, when we were going to do it. We had overlooked the fact that his clinic would be full of dogs already being boarded for the holiday weekend, and we were fixin' to show up with forty-one dogs from the pounds in need of all kinds of care. But, thankfully, Dr. Hoegemeyer accepted all forty-one dogs over that weekend and never let on what we had done to him and his clinic.

On the morning of Friday, September 4th, I left Utopia in my old 1981 Chevy pickup and headed to Kerrville to meet up with Marcie and her friend Molly McCoy to rescue the dogs from the Kerrville pound. We had absolutely no idea how many dogs were waiting to be rescued from death row. At eleven o'clock I met up with them at the pound in Kerrville; Marcie was in her red convertible and Molly was driving a Suburban. I parked my old truck, Trigger, at the back of the pound near the dog pens.

The three of us went inside the pound office, introduced ourselves, and told them we wanted to rescue all of the dogs that they had. The people who worked at the pound were more than delighted to assist us and took us to the barking dogs in the back.

One by one, we leashed and walked (or carried) the dogs out to our vehicles and put them in cages. What took place at the pound was incredible to me—the dogs actually knew what was going on. They knew they were being rescued and all seemed to be grateful to us.

With approximately ten dogs loaded up, we drove the one mile slowly over to Hoegemeyer Animal Clinic where Kinky was waiting for us outside. He helped us unload the dogs and get them inside. The instructions were for the veterinarians to give the dogs a checkup, test for heartworms, spay and neuter, worm, and give rabies shots and anything else that they needed. Looking back, now I realize why the staff at the clinic seemed to be a little bit shocked, to say the least.

After we had unloaded we took off again for the pound to reload. This time Marcie chose to ride with me. We were both very excited about what was happening and could not wait to grab some more dogs. The employees at the pound had already leashed up ten more dogs for us to take and were waiting for us outside as we pulled up. After loading Molly's Suburban and my truck we had room for one more dog inside my truck, because Marcie wanted to ride in the back of the truck with the caged dogs.

A scared black Chow mix with a soft, raspy voice barked at me, so I went over to his cage and tried to put a leash on him. He seemed to be happy but refused to let me put a collar on him, so I bent down and picked him up. I decided to name him Curly right then and there. Mr. Curly clung to me tightly and showered me with kisses all the way back to the truck. I put him inside the cab and climbed in. He was so happy to be rescued that he sat in my lap and wouldn't budge an inch.

Once again, we headed to Hoegemeyer Animal Clinic with Marcie in the back of my truck singing to the happy dogs and me with Curly sitting in my lap, helping me drive. Once again, Kinky was outside the clinic waiting for us, and thank goodness that he was, because he ended up saving his little sister Marcie's life!

As soon as I had parked Trigger at the clinic, this giant dog that we had named Hearty decided to leap out of the back of my truck. His leash was wrapped around Marcie's waist, and when he jumped out the leash nearly cut Marcie in two. Luckily, Kinky grabbed Hearty and lifted the one-hundred-and-twenty-pound canine safely back inside the back of the truck, giving Marcie enough time to remove the leash from around her waist.

One by one, we unloaded the dogs at the clinic. The last to go in on this trip was Mr. Curly. I had to carry this clinging, forty-pound dog inside and needed help from the staff at the clinic to pull him off of me because he wouldn't let go.

Once again, we departed for the pound. We left Kinky in charge at the clinic to visit with the rescued dogs and reassure them that they were going to be fine.

When we arrived back at the pound, a couple of old people were inside the office signing surrender papers on their dog, knowing all too well that he would be killed within a few days. The reason they were dumping this dog was that he had eaten one of their Social Security checks, and they were mad. The three of us stood there in the lobby in shock—not believing what we had just heard—and we were mad. As soon as the couple had left the building, Marcie asked the personnel if we could take the dog. The answer was an immediate yes. We named him Cat, because he was part Catahoula, and then we loaded him up. Later that day, I said to Kinky, "I wonder if they would have done that if it had been a phone or an electric bill?"

We were outside loading dogs when one of the pound trucks pulled up near the back of the building and unloaded a big dog that had just been hit by a car. We were told that the pound was going to kill her immediately and put her out of her misery.

Once again, Marcie came to the rescue and asked if we could take her. The answer was yes. Marcie put the dog in the back seat of her convertible and took off for the clinic like she had been shot out of a cannon. Molly and I finished up getting the rest of the dogs and left the pound completely empty of dogs.

When we arrived at the clinic, Kinky told us that Marcie had named the dog that had just been hit by a car Choula, and that the dog was pregnant and had just miscarried. Five of the puppies were dead, with only one survivor, and they weren't sure if the little fella was going to make it. He then told us that Dr. Hoegemeyer was doing surgery right then on Choula, who had multiple fractures and a broken hip, and the prognosis wasn't good, either. Saddened by Kinky's news, I drove back home to Utopia and said little prayers for Choula and her puppy.

The next morning Kinky called to tell us that Choula and the puppy were in stable condition and that Marcie had gone back to the pound and rescued all of the dogs that were there this morning. He told me that one of the dogs Marcie rescued was a Border Collie with four six-week-old pups, and she had named the mama dog Fly. And, after Marcie had loaded Fly in her car and had gone back to get her puppies, Fly jumped out of Marcie's car and raced back inside the pound to protect them. It ended up that the staff helped Marcie carry the puppies to her car with Fly right by their side, keeping a constant, watchful eye on them.

After Kinky and I hung up, my phone rang again. It was Dr. Hoegemeyer calling to tell me that Hearty, the giant dog who had nearly cut Marcie in two, had heartworms and needed to be treated immediately. I told him to go ahead and treat him, and to do anything else that he felt any of our dogs needed.

Early Sunday morning, I met up with my friend Knoxie Johnson at the Hondo pound to help rescue more dogs. Knoxie is an angel and the founder and director of the Uvalde Animal Shelter, a no-kill shelter for dogs and cats. She had heard about some dogs that needed rescuing over in Hondo and asked us to help.

Tony told me that the rescue ranch had space available for about four more dogs, so I took a female Chow and her puppy and named her Lucille Ball and her son Bear. I also took a red, medium-sized mutt and named him Fred, and two other small dogs which I named Peanut and Tuffy. Knoxie took the rest back to Uvalde, and I drove my five to Hoegemeyer Animal Clinic for checkups, neutering, and shots.

The total number of dogs rescued during that "Labor Dog" weekend had now reached forty-one—we were full and so was Dr. Bill Hoegemeyer's clinic!

Dr. Hoegemeyer and Dr. Jay Rydberg at the clinic were spaying or neutering or treating our dogs for ailments every day. They averaged two to four of our dogs a day, and eventually all of the dogs were gone from the clinic and living on our ranch.

On one visit, when we picked up Curly, I found out that his larynx had been broken and that was why his bark was raspy and muffled, and also why he hated dog collars. I guess someone must have tried to choke him, or maybe he was injured when he was captured by a dog-catcher. The last two dogs to leave the clinic from that first rescue were Choula, who survived her surgeries, and her precious pup, Roscoe, who Tony named.

Slowly but surely we began adopting out our dogs. As a selling tool, I would tell each potential adopter that the dog that they had picked out to adopt was one of our "Magnificent Seven"—meaning one of the first seven dogs that we had rescued. This really helped with the adoptions, and everyone seemed really proud to know that they had chosen one of the first of seven dogs that we had ever rescued.

Over six months had passed when on one of Kinky's visits to the rescue ranch he asked me in a serious tone, "Nance, how many of the original 'Magnificent Seven' do we have left?"

"About twenty-one," I answered.

And to anyone who thinks that they may have adopted one of our "Magnificent Seven" dogs—you did, because we believe that all dogs are magnificent!

The "Magnificent Seven"

1. Maxwell Smart: Black Lab mix—male, approx. 3 years old
2. Hearty: Giant gray mutt—male, approx. 4 years old
3. Happy: Black & white mutt—male, approx. 3 years old
4. Joy: Small black & white mutt—female, approx. 3 years old
5. Amigo: Med. blue merle Aussie mix—male, approx. 3 months old
6. Blue: Med. blue merle Aussie mix—male, approx. 3 months old
7. Candy: Med. blue merle Aussie mix—female, approx. 3 months old
8. Jasper: Giant red mutt—male, approx. 2 years old
9. Carmella: Giant red mutt—female, approx. 2 years old
10. Rocky: Rottweiler—male, approx. 1 year old
11. Cat: Catahoula—male, approx. 2 years old (ate owner's Social Security check)
12. Fly: Border Collie—female, approx. 6 years old (came with her four puppies)
13. Curly: Black Chow mix—male, approx. 3 years old
14. Red: Red Heeler—male, approx. 4 years old
15. Molly: Collie mix—female, approx. 3 years old
16. Magic: Black Lab—female, approx. 4 months old
17. Frosty: Furry giant—male, approx. 2 years old
18. Fred: Red Chow mix—male, approx. 6 months old
19. Gus: Black Lab—male, approx. 1 year old
20. Alice: Golden Retriever—female, approx. 2 years old

21. Loretta: Red Heeler mix—female, approx. 2 years old
22. Prissy: Blue Heeler mix—female, approx. 3 years old
23. Fritz: Schnauzer mix—male, approx. 2 years old
24. Lucille Ball: Red Chow—female, approx. 4 years old
25. Bear: Red Chow—male, approx. 3 months old (Lucy's kid)
26. Peanut: Small wiry mutt—male, approx. 4 months old
27. Tuffy: Small wiry mutt—male, approx. 4 months old
28. Vinnie: Big white mutt—male, approx. 1 year old
29. Jack: Rat Terrier—male, approx. 6 years old
30. Spanky: Rat Terrier—male, approx. 3 years old
31. Roscoe: Boxer mix—male, born at vet clinic before Choula's surgery (Choula's pup)
32. Choula: Blue Heeler mix—female, approx. 3 years old (hit by car; Roscoe's mom)
33. Dan: Black Lab mix—male, approx. 5 years old
34. Sue: Pit Bull mix—female, approx. 3 years old
35. Dorothy: Red Heeler mix—female, approx. 2 years old
36. Smokey: Black Lab mix—male, approx. 8 years old
37. Vincent Van Friedman: Schnauzer mix—male, approx. 2 years old

*Plus Fly's four puppies

"Pryor-itized"

Pretty Mama

Jo and Willow West

PART TWO

Meanwhile, Back at
the Ranch

My Furry Angel

Peanut, the hero dog

Ben Stiller, looking for love

Boomer

"Luck-A-Luck"

Mirror, Mirror on the Wall

In the summer of 1996, before we had officially started the Utopia Animal Rescue Ranch, Tony and I rescued two ducks that some people in Utopia no longer could keep because they were moving. We named the ducks Kathy and Harry, in honor of our friends Kathy Thornburg and Dr. Harry Barnard.

When we brought the ducks to our ranch, Tony and I set them free at the barn and then had to walk them down to the big stock tank so they could go swimming. Instead of going into the water to swim like most ducks would, they marched off toward the barn. We figured that they just wanted to check out the place first and then go back to the tank to swim, so we didn't think much about it.

Every hour or so I would anxiously look out the trailer window to see if the ducks had returned to the stock tank. Nope—still no ducks in the water.

Tony and I couldn't figure out why our ducks didn't want to go to the stock tank to swim. So after lunch, Tony went to the barn and herded Harry and Kathy back down to the stock tank, but as soon as he got them down to the water and left them alone, they immediately marched right back up to the barn.

Texas summers are usually not the most pleasant time of the year down here, and Tony and I were stumped why our rescued ducks preferred staying in the old hot barn instead of the cool of the water.

Two days passed and the ducks still stayed in the barn and never left it. I was ready to call the veterinarian to come out and examine the ducks to see what was the matter with them, but Tony suggested that we call our friend Maribeth Couch first.

Maribeth loves birds and she is great with them. Tony wanted to see if she had any ideas or brilliant suggestions before calling in a bird psychologist or veterinarian. So Tony called Maribeth and told her about the ducks' odd behavior and asked her if she had any thoughts about it. She asked Tony if we had anything shiny laying round in the barn, like a mirror. She explained to Tony that if a bird sees his reflection he won't leave it, because he thinks it is part of the flock. Tony told her he didn't think we had anything out there but promised her that we would go out to the barn and check immediately. Thank goodness Tony had called Maribeth!

As soon as Tony hung up the phone, we went to the barn. When we entered it Kathy and Harry didn't seem to even notice us, because they were too busy standing in front of a discarded door mirror—staring intensely into it and appearing to be mesmerized.

After Tony and I had quit laughing, he immediately picked up the old mirror and laid it face down on the top of some nearby barrels. To our amazement, Harry and Kathy looked at each other, and then waddled side-by-side out of the barn and headed straight for our stock tank! As soon as the ducks arrived at the stock tank they took off swimming and never returned to the barn again.

Soon, all of our dogs grew accustomed to the ducks, and old Thunder, our crippled black Lab, began sleeping with them. When Kinky's dog, Mr. Magoo, came to stay with us while Kinky was on a book tour, he did not know what to think about the new ducks. Gooie wasn't exactly scared of Kathy and Harry, but he was very curious about them. Tony and I even caught him chasing them a few times the first day that he had met them.

The day after Mr. Magoo had come to stay with us, Gooie learned to respect Harry and Kathy—thanks to Kathy. Tony was outside and I was inside the trailer when I heard Gooie's yelp followed by a loud thump underneath the floor. I rushed outside to see what was going on, and there was Tony standing by the porch holding Mr. Magoo in his arms and laughing.

Tony told me that he would tell me everything if I would go get the medicine kit, because Gooie had a large cut on the top of his nose that was starting to bleed. When I returned with the kit, Tony told me, as he doctored Goo's nose, that Gooie had been sleeping peaceably under the trailer, when Kathy walked up behind him and goosed him in the rear end, startling Mr. Magoo, causing him to jump up and bang his nose under the trailer.

As soon as Goo had been doctored, he ran into the trailer acting somewhat embarrassed. From that day on, Gooie would have nothing to do with our ducks. Anytime that Kathy or Harry showed up in the front yard Goo would magically disappear.

As time marched on, Tony caught Kathy several times goosing one of our sleeping dogs. Within two months of the ducks' arrival at the ranch, all of our dogs showed Kathy and Harry respect. In fact, when our dogs went swimming in the stock tank they always followed Kathy and Harry from a far, safe distance.

When Kinky, Tony, and I started the rescue ranch, we made Kathy one of its mascots. When visitors would arrive, she would always waddle up and be the first to greet them. Even though our rescue ranch dogs didn't ever get goosed by Kathy, they must have picked up on Tony's and my dogs' behavior, because they would never bark at her if she came up to the front yard to visit.

Soon, with all of the new traffic coming and going from the newly founded rescue ranch Kathy became our personal alarm system. Any car that came down our dirt road (except for ours) would start Kathy quacking wildly to alert us. She was very helpful to have around.

One cool fall morning in 1999, Tony came inside the trailer to tell me that Kathy had died. Tony found her near the water, down by the stock tank, with Harry standing guard beside her as if to protect her. Tony tried to get Harry to go back into the water, but he would not leave her side.

Anyone who questions the love and soul of an animal should have seen Harry standing by his best friend for over an hour, before Tony could bury her. It was heartfelt and very touching.

After burying Kathy, Tony carved a small piece of wood to mark her grave with these words: "Kathy the Toughest Duck in Texas 1996–1999."

To Be So Lucky

The first time Kinky called us about an animal that he had rescued, it wasn't a dog—it was a kitten.

In August 1996, Kinky and his friend Mike McGovern were driving down Highway 16 headed for Kerrville to eat lunch. Kinky caught a glimpse of something on the side of the road and stopped to check it out. What he and Mike found was a bloody, weak eight-week-old kitten that had been shot in the front leg by some great white hunter. The kitten was almost dead.

Kinky and McGovern rushed him to Dr. Hoegemeyer's animal clinic in Kerrville to see what could be done. Dr. Hoegemeyer's initial prognosis wasn't good. He told Kinky and Mike that because the kitten was so weak from dehydration and blood loss he probably would not survive the operating table. He then asked Kinky what he wanted him to do.

After hearing the kitten's poor prognosis, it only took Kinky one second to decide what should be done. He knew that the odds were against this little kitten surviving, with or without the operation, so he decided to take the gamble—the kitten would have the operation.

It is said that cats have nine lives. Well, this little wannabe cat was now down to eight and still counting down. Dr. Hoegemeyer told Kinky, after performing the two-hour operation on the kitten, that his little patient had actually died on the operating table when his right front leg was amputated, but fortunately he was able to revive him back. Dr. Hoegemeyer also warned Kinky not to get his hopes up yet, because the next forty-eight hours would be critical in determining whether the three-legged kitten would live or die.

For Kinky, forty-eight hours can be a very, very long time, or it can fly by faster than a hurricane headed toward the Astrodome. In this scenario, Houston did not have a problem. For the next few days Kinky was either at the clinic checking up on his new little friend or calling the clinic to get an update on his condition. Thankfully, the little kitten was growing stronger by the hour and his chances for survival were slowly climbing.

By day three, the kitten had beaten the odds of his prognosis, and Dr.

Hoegemeyer phoned Kinky to tell him the good news. Kinky and Mike were overjoyed with his report and drove immediately to Kerrville to pick up the kitten and bring him back to Kinky's home, which is called the Lodge on Echo Hill Ranch in Medina, Texas. On their twenty-one-mile drive to the clinic Kinky decided to name the kitten Morgan in honor of a deceased close friend.

After they arrived at Hoegemeyer Animal Clinic, Dr. Hoegemeyer handed Kinky and Mike about five or six bottles of medicine that the little kitten needed daily. He showed them how to clean and dress the wound and apply ointments and then told them when to give Morgan his many pills. Before departing for the Lodge, Kinky wrote out a check for over one thousand dollars to cover Morgan's medical bills.

For several days, Mike and Kinky took turns nursing Morgan back to health. Day by day, the young feline seemed to grow stronger and healthier. After about a week of this, Kinky called to tell me that he and Mike were joining Willie Nelson in Mexico for a short vacation before Kinky had to go on the road to kick off his new book tour. He wanted to know if Tony and I could babysit his rescued Lab mix, Mr. Magoo, and his newly rescued kitten, Morgan, for about eight weeks.

Even though I had never had a kitten or a cat, my answer was yes, but I was a little bit skeptical. I worried about it dying while in my care, and then being labeled a cat killer by Kinky for the rest of my life. I made Kinky promise me that if the kitten were to die while he was gone that he would not blame or hate me.

After leaving Kinky's ranch with Morgan, with Mr. Magoo riding shotgun on the front seat, I had a little talk with the kitten before arriving back at my ranch. I explained to him about my never having had a cat before and told him that he needed to be patient with me. I also promised him that Tony and I would do our best to take care of him and then begged Morgan not to go and die on me while Kinky was gone. My final request of him was to please not be the kind of cat that pounces on me from out of nowhere when I'm least expecting it, because it could cause me to have an unwanted heart attack. In this case, as often as it is with Kinky's cases, the cat said nothing.

Upon our arrival back at Rolling Thunder Ranch, my mini-ranch in Utopia, the three of us were greeted by Tony and our dogs Thunder, Yoda, Chili, Little Girl, and Hank. After Mr. Magoo and our dogs had said their hellos to each other by sniffing each other's butts, their attention was then turned to the cat that sat inside of Tony's cowboy hat.

Following a brief introduction, Tony carried Morgan to my office inside our trailer. He and I had decided earlier to use my office because it had a Dutch door. We would be able to look in on him without disturbing him, and the bottom door would be kept closed to keep our dogs out.

Morgan needed more care than Tony and I had anticipated. If Tony wasn't cleaning or feeding him, I was giving him a pill or applying various ointments to his wound. In other words, Morgan's medical needs were around the clock.

Kinky called us daily to check on Morgan and Mr. Magoo. Our reports were always the same: "Morgan is doing fabulous!" As the weeks rolled by, Morgan grew stronger and healthier. His wound had healed beautifully and new fur had grown in to completely cover his scar. And as the time passed, Tony and I and our dogs fell in love with Morgan. We considered him family, but I did have one problem with him: it was his name; it didn't fit him. Tony and I found ourselves calling him all kinds of different names, but never Morgan.

The next time that I spoke to Kinky I asked him if he would consider letting me rename Morgan. I told him that Tony and I had found ourselves calling Morgan Lucky Cat, Luck-a-Luck, or just plain Lucky. I told Kinky that Tony and I wanted to change his name to Lucky, because he was one of the luckiest cats alive. First, for being rescued, then for surviving a surgery that he shouldn't have survived, and now, being one of Kinky's cats, for having the best life any cat could wish for.

Kinky liked my idea, especially because John McCall had just suggested to him that he name the kitten Lucky. Since Kinky was outnumbered three-to-one, he agreed to the name change. Morgan was now Lucky!

A week before the end of Kinky's book tour, Kinky's father, Dr. Tom Friedman, had a serious heart attack in Austin. Fortunately, he survived it. When Tom was released from the hospital to go home, Kinky decided to stay with him in Austin until he had fully recuperated. That took two months.

Once Tom was back in the saddle and had fully recovered, Kinky returned home to his Lodge at Echo Hill Ranch, after being gone for nearly four months. I must admit that I had mixed emotions about Kinky's homecoming. I couldn't wait to see Kinky because I had missed him, but was depressed knowing that Lucky would be leaving with Mr. Magoo.

When Kinky arrived at his Lodge, the first thing he did was phone us to ask us to bring Mr. Magoo and Lucky to him—he couldn't wait to see them! While Kinky was unpacking, Tony and I were packing. We packed up Magoo's many balls and toys and Lucky's five fake dead mice into their old black duffel bag that had "Friedman" embroidered on the side of it.

Tony was not too thrilled to see them leave, nor was I. On our forty-two mile trip over to Echo Hill Ranch, Lucky rode silently beside me in the front seat of our pickup while Gooie rode shotgun and yapped with excitement the entire forty-five minutes. After reuniting Kinky with his furry family, I drove back home in silence because the truck's radio was broken.

When I arrived back at Rolling Thunder Ranch, I became really depressed when I went inside my catless trailer—it felt empty without Lucky there. Later that evening Tony and I had a little talk. We decided that we needed a cat and made plans to go to the pound in Uvalde the following morning to rescue a cat that would hopefully be as great as Luck-a-Luck.

Well, forget that. Just after dawn, the following morning, Tony and I received one of the best phone calls that we have ever received.

"Cousin Nancy, this is Kinky," he said, sounding rather irritated.

"Yes?"

"Could you please get over here as soon as possible and pick up this crazy cat?"

"Sure," I said, smiling ear to ear. "Why? What's going on over there?"

"Has Lucky ever bitten you?" Kinky asked.

"No, never," I answered. "Why?"

"Well, he has been scratching and biting me ever since you left yesterday. He hates it over here, and I'm going to bleed to death if you don't get over here soon!"

"Are you serious?" I asked, trying not to laugh.

"Yes, I'm serious," Kinky stated. "Do you want him or not?"

"I'm on my way, Kinky. Do you want me to bring you some Band-Aids?"

Kinky answered, "Yes, and hurry!"

After hanging up the phone and grabbing my first aid kit, I told Tony as I was going out the front door that Lucky was coming back to us for good, and I was fixin' to go pick him up.

As I climbed into our pickup, Tony asked me why I was taking our first aid kit with me and all I could do was laugh.

"Don't ask. I'll tell you later."

When I arrived at Kinky's, I was taken aback. Kinky, Lucky, and Magoo were standing outside the Lodge ready to greet me. In all my life I have never simultaneously had a big, black dog, a three-legged cat, and a man with a cigar be so glad to see me! Gooie rushed to me with a tennis ball in his mouth, Lucky leaped up into my arms and began kissing me, and Kinky just stood there by the gate covered with scratch marks, smoking a cigar and smiling.

Following a quick cup of strong Kona coffee and a brief visit with Kinky, I happily placed Lucky on the front seat of the pickup and drove him home. As soon as I got Lucky inside my trailer, Tony and I sat him down on the bench in the "great room" (14' × 12'), and I told him that I was so glad to have him back and promised him that I would never do that to him again.

Lucky gave me his full attention and seemed to understand what I was saying to him. The whole time that I was apologizing to him, he just sat still on the bench, staring deeply into my eyes. When I told him that I was finished apologizing, he bit me hard on the chin! It hurt like you-know-what, but I had to laugh. I deserved it. Lucky had just proven to me that the old saying that "cats don't get mad—they get even" was totally true.

With my chin bleeding profusely, I asked Tony to please drive to town to buy us another emergency first aid kit because I had left ours over at Kinky's. As soon as Tony drove off to town, I phoned Kinky to inform him that I had just been bitten by Lucky. We had a good laugh about it. Then we agreed that the reason Lucky had bitten us was because he had bonded with Tony's and my family, and that was why he had bitten and scratched Kinky within an inch of his life and had gotten even with me afterwards.

Lucky has now lived with Tony and me for ten years and has never once pounced on me or bitten me ever again. At night Tony and I sleep with Lucky and our seven dogs in our bed. Our dogs take turns during the night sleeping on our bed with us, but not Luck-a-Luck; he is a constant.

Lucky's best friend is our old, lame black Labrador, Thunder, that Tony and I rescued years ago. They are inseparable. She and Lucky spend their daytime hours either sleeping side by side on the couch or licking and kissing one another.

Since then, Kinky, Tony, and I have made Lucky one of our official mascots for our rescue ranch because he was our first rescue together. We are also proud to say that Lucky has single-handedly killed two baby rattlesnakes and more mice than we care to count. He is an incredible cat and we feel that we are so lucky that he chose the three of us to share his life with.

Good Golly, Miss Molly

Marcie and I rescued Molly from the Kerrville pound on Labor Day Weekend. She was one of the "Magnificent Seven." When we went to her cage to rescue her, we found a medium-sized, long-haired black dog with tan markings on her muzzle and head. She was scared and frightened of us. She had obviously been abused and she didn't want anything to do with us or anyone else; she did not trust people.

On the drive over to the clinic, Molly shook horribly and jerked away when I tried to pet her. She was scared to death. I spoke softly to her, trying to calm her, but her trembling continued for the entire trip. When we arrived at the clinic, I had to carry this forty-five-pound bundle of nerves to her cage. I didn't want to leave her, but I had to go back to the pound to get more dogs. As I was leaving, Kinky pulled up to the clinic. I told him about Molly and took him to see her. She was curled up in the corner of her cage, shivering, and wouldn't even look at us. Somebody had really done her wrong. Kinky was very concerned about her and stayed with her in her cage for nearly an hour before leaving the clinic.

Molly was spayed a few days later, given a clean bill of health, and was now ready for us to come and take her to her new home in Utopia. Having heard the story about Molly, Tony decided before we brought her to our ranch that she should be Curly's roommate, and they would share the Willie Nelson Pen.

Curly, the one with the raspy bark, was a sweet, gentle medium-sized black wannabe Border Collie. He, too, was one of our "Magnificent Seven" that had been abused and mistreated. Tony's decision to pair the two was right—they made for a good match. Curly and Molly became fast friends. They shared their food and a doghouse to sleep in at night, even though there were two doghouses in their pen.

Tony, who has a special touch with animals, knew that with Curly's help he could turn Molly around in time. Three or four times every day, Tony would go to Molly and Curly's pen and sit with them. Curly would run to Tony to greet him, and Molly would watch from a distance. Then Tony would sit near Molly with Curly in his lap. Slowly, Molly began to trust Tony, with the help of Curly, and seemed to perk up especially when he was around. It seemed that Molly and Curly had let Tony join their inner circle of friends.

After a couple of weeks, Molly would take Curly's cue and race him to greet Tony. That was a giant breakthrough for her. Within that same week, Tony had Molly sitting in his lap and giving him kisses. A very special bond had now formed between Tony and Molly—it was love and trust. At the rescue ranch, we all try not to have favorites or show favoritism, but it was clear to everyone that Tony loved Molly and she loved him.

Months and months passed by and Miss Molly kept being overlooked for adoption. Tony really wanted to adopt her, but our trailer was overflowing with rescued dogs and cats already. On several occasions, when someone came out to possibly adopt one of our dogs, Molly would become very shy and go into her doghouse to hide from the visitors. A couple of times, the would-be adopters made remarks to us about her shyness. It was as though she didn't want to be adopted or leave the rescue ranch.

On Valentine's Day 1999, Kinky drove over to the rescue ranch to bring a young woman to see the ranch, because she had told Kinky that she might consider adopting one of our dogs. Tony gave the young woman a tour. When they arrived at Curly's and Molly's pen, the two dogs raced to the gate to greet Tony. Before Tony could say a word the young woman told him that she wanted to adopt Molly.

Kinky and I were excited about Molly's adoption, but Tony didn't feel good about it at all. I thought he was just sad and didn't want to let her go—oh boy, was I ever wrong about that.

After signing the adoption papers, Tony sadly loaded up Molly into Kinky's car, and Kinky and the young woman left the rescue ranch with Molly in the back seat shaking. After they left, Tony went out to the pens to check on the dogs. When he returned to our trailer, I could tell that he had been crying but did not say a word.

Over the weeks that followed, Tony voiced his concerns many times about Molly and how worried he was about her. Well, come to find out, Tony's concerns should not have been taken lightly. One of Kinky's friends up in Austin, whom Kinky had asked to check up on Molly, had informed Kinky that Molly was not working out well in her new home. His friend told him that we needed to get Molly back—she was in bad hands. I have never seen Tony so upset as he was after Kinky called us to tell us the news about Molly. He was ready to drive our nineteen-year-old pickup up to Austin and rescue her right then! Thank goodness Kinky called back before Tony left.

Kinky wanted to talk to Tony, so I put Tony on the phone with him. Kinky told Tony that it was not necessary to go to Austin, because he had already set the wheels in motion to rescue Molly. He told Tony that his friend Kay Cavin, the woman who had checked up on Molly and informed him about her situation, was now on her way over to the young woman's house to rescue Molly and would call us as soon as Kay had Molly.

It seemed like a year had passed, but it had only been a little under an hour when Kinky phoned the rescue ranch. Tony took the call. It was good news—Molly had just been rescued and was now on her way to Kay's house! Kinky went on to tell Tony that Kay told him the woman had no problem giving Miss Molly up to her, and she told Kay that she thought Molly was brain damaged because every time that she would sit down, Molly would come over and try to sit beside her. She also told Kay that she really didn't like Molly that much after all.

Kay had heard enough! She put a leash on Molly and they left the young woman's house. Molly shook all of the way to Kay's house, but when she met Kay's daughter, Rachel, her tail went up, and she quit quivering and gave Rachel a kiss!

The following day, Tony called Kay to check on Molly and arrange for a pick-up time to bring Molly back to the rescue ranch. Kay told Tony to forget it. She and Rachel had fallen in love with Molly and wanted to adopt her, because Molly had slept all night in Rachel's bed with her and their cat and she was now outside in the backyard playing ball with Rachel.

This was both good and bad news for Tony. He really wanted Molly back, but, knowing that Molly was really happy, he told Kay that they could have her on one condition. She and Rachel had to promise to bring Molly back to the rescue ranch for visits. Kay agreed to Tony's request, and Molly was now officially adopted to a super home!

A few weeks later, Kinky, Kay, Rachel, and Molly came out for a visit to the rescue ranch, as promised. Tony was so excited about seeing Molly he forgot to introduce himself to Kay and Rachel when they pulled up to the trailer and parked.

When Molly got out of their car she ran straight to Tony and gave him a kiss—her tail never stopped wagging. We visited for a little while and then had a picnic outside. Molly sat between Rachel and Tony on one side of the picnic table, and the three of us sat across from them. Tony and Rachel took turns feeding Molly their picnic lunches as Kinky, Kay, and I watched with enjoyment.

After lunch, Rachel and Kay decided to go for a walk on the ranch with Molly. As Tony watched them walking, he commented that Molly seemed to be really happy and noticed that she had not once left Rachel's side the entire time of their walk. At last, Tony felt good about

Molly and her new family—she had finally found her angels, and Kay and Rachel had found theirs.

On July 5, 1999, Kinky called our ranch to tell us that Molly was dead. Kay had just called him, crying with the sad news. On the night of July 4th, she and Rachel had gone to a Fourth of July picnic, and while they were gone the neighbors started shooting off fireworks. Molly must have been terrified and escaped from the backyard. When Kay and Rachel returned home they found Molly dead in the street. She had been hit by a car.

They were devastated and so were we—especially Tony.

Peanut: Don't Leave Home without Her!

Peanut, a small, fuzzy little female dog, was one of the "Magnificent Seven." She only weighed about ten pounds but had a personality as big as Texas. Tony had named her Peanut but often called her his "little clown." Peanut's best friend, Tuffy, was a little male mutt about the same size as her. The two of them were inseparable—they were either playing or sleeping together.

In December 1998, Kinky brought his friend Kacey Jones from Nashville, Tennessee, over to the rescue ranch to show her around and hopefully get her to adopt one of our dogs. Kacey fell in love with all of our dogs—especially Peanut.

She wanted to adopt Peanut right then and there but the timing wasn't right, so she asked us to hold Peanut for her until she got back home to Nashville. Kinky, Tony, and I were delighted and promised Kacey that we would hold on to Peanut for her.

Two weeks later, Kacey called from Nashville. She was now ready to adopt Peanut. The only way we could get Peanut to Nashville was to fly her, so I called my friend Wendi Paschal, who worked for American Airlines. Months earlier, when Wendi had come out to visit our ranch with her husband, Ed, and friend Antoinette, she made us an offer that we couldn't refuse. Her offer was to fly any of our dogs anywhere that American flew—for free!

When I told Wendi that we needed her help to fly Peanut to Nashville, her answer was an immediate yes. Within the hour, Wendi had booked Peanut's flight, and all of the arrangements had been taken care of. Wendi even called Kacey to confirm Peanut's flight and to tell her that she had found a stewardess to accompany Peanut on the flight— Peanut would be flying first class to Nashville! And, to top that, Peanut would be hand-delivered to her when they landed in Nashville.

On January 23, 1999, Tony and I drove Peanut to the San Antonio airport to deliver Peanut to the stewardess at American Airlines. It turned out that the stewardess was a steward named James Hill. He was a nice young man who fell in love with Peanut immediately. While holding Peanut in his arms, he told us that she would be flying first class out to Nashville, either sitting in the seat beside him or on his lap. He told us that there was no need for the crate and gave it back to us.

We said our good-byes to Peanut and thanked James for helping us get Peanut safely out to Nashville, and then we left the airport. Later that afternoon, Kacey called to thank us and to tell us that she and Peanut had bonded and were doing great. She also told us that James told her that Peanut had stolen everyone's heart on the plane and had been a little clown the entire trip to Nashville.

Every week we received reports on Peanut from Kacey. It sounded like Peanut was spoiled to death and living the life of Riley; we loved hearing that kind of news.

On February 1, 1999, Peanut's friend, Tuffy, got adopted to a great home, so Tony went to the Kerrville pound and rescued two dogs from death row to put into Peanut's and Tuffy's old pen. We named one of the dogs Kacey Jones, in honor of Kacey for adopting Peanut, and the other dog we named Spot.

About a month after Peanut had flown out to Nashville, Kacey called the rescue ranch to tell us that Peanut was a Nashville hero, and she had just saved her life! She told me the story and said that she had already posted it up on her website: kinkajourecords.com. I went to her website, and this is an excerpt from her story:

The True Story of Peanut "The Hero Dog" Jones
or How I Was Rescued by a Rescue Ranch Dog

By Kacey Jones

About a month after her arrival, Peanut and I walked down to the local ATM machine to get some fast cash. It was a Saturday night, it was after dark, and yes, I know it was a stupid thing to do. I live in the Music Row area of Nashville. On the weekends, most of the buildings empty out, their music biz tenants fleeing to the suburbs. The only ones left walking the Row at night are a few unemployed songwriters and a bunch of deliriously insane derelicts, who are often mistaken for unemployed songwriters, and me and Peanut.

I put my card into the ATM machine, but the machine didn't give me any money, and it ate my card. I hate when that happens. Highly agitated, I stuck my hand back into my empty pocket and suggested to Peanut we go home and order a pizza with our credit card. We headed back to my apartment by way of the Vanderbilt campus. It was raining so I had my umbrella in my right hand and Peanut on the leash in my left.

When we reached the campus area, I let Peanut off the leash so she could run for awhile. Just as I let her go, a man wearing a hooded sweatshirt, sweat pants, white socks, and surfer sandals came from out of nowhere and grabbed my left arm. It hurt my arm, it scared me, and it pissed me off. "What'd ya got in your pocket?!" he demanded. I struggled to loosen his grip and get my left hand free so I could grab hold of the coach's whistle I was wearing around my neck. My Grandma Myrtle gave it to me years ago; it had an eardrum shattering blast and I hoped it would send the nearest cop running to my rescue. But there weren't any cops around that night.

I began flailing my assailant with my umbrella, beating him over his hooded head while still trying to free my left hand. Suddenly, Peanut came charging up. Courageously, she sunk her little teeth into the fleshy part of the perpetrator's sandaled foot, causing him enough pain and distraction to let go of my left arm. I grabbed Grandma Myrtle's whistle and started blowing my brains out. It must have been quite a picture. Me, beating the guy over the head with an umbrella and blowing that whistle in his face, and all the while Peanut barking her little brindle colored head off.

Fortunately, the guy never brandished a weapon. In what appeared to be utter frustration, he ran off into the night leaving me and Peanut standing there, shaken but victorious.

I cannot explain to you why a little dog who had lived with me barely a month had the instinct to know I was in danger and the fortitude to come to my rescue. What I can tell you is this . . . before you consider buying an expensive "purebred" dog, give serious consideration to adopting a Rescue Ranch dog. Their gratitude will come back to you in spades . . . make that, aces.

Sincerely,
Kacey Jones

P.S. The last song on my new CD is entitled "Peanut Sonata." Peanut sang the back-up vocals. It's her recording debut. She did great.

The following week we received Kacey's CD. It sounded great—especially "Peanut Sonata."

Remember the Alamo!

Over a year had passed since Peanut's flight when I received a sad call from Wendi Paschal at American Airlines. She started out asking how Peanut was doing in Nashville and wound up crying when she told me that she and her husband, Ed, wanted to adopt a dog from us because their dog, Dolly, had just died. They knew that Dolly would want them to bring another dog into their home so it could be loved the way Dolly had been loved.

Wendi asked us to pick out a dog for them. The only qualifications she had were that the dog be a female, at least two years old, and have at least three legs and a tail. She told me that as soon as we had picked one out for them they would fly down to San Antonio and pick her up at the airport.

This was the first and only time that Tony and I had ever been asked to pick out a dog and "mail" it to someone. We went outside and, after looking at all of our dogs, we decided on Kacey Jones—forgetting that Wendi had helped us fly Peanut to Kacey over a year ago. We returned to our trailer and I called Wendi and told her about Kacey Jones.

On April 15, 2000, at 5:30 in the morning, our good friend Lindy Padgett drove Kacey Jones to the San Antonio airport to deliver her to Wendi and Ed. That evening Wendi called to tell me that they were in love with Kacey Jones, but she and Ed had decided to change her name to Alamo. She told me that Alamo was getting along fine with their other dog and thanked Tony and me for choosing her.

Wendi also teased me about sending them a one-year-old dog instead of a two-year-old one and for sending them a dog with no tail, which she had requested in her over-the-phone dog order. I explained that since Alamo had all four legs, I figured that they could deal with her not having a tail.

From time to time, Wendi would call or send us a note telling us about Alamo's antics. Thank goodness that she and Ed are animal lovers, each having a great sense of humor and more importantly—credit cards.

The first unusual thing they noticed about Alamo, besides her not having a tail, was that she hikes her leg, like a male dog, when she urinates. When they asked their veterinarian about it he told them he had never heard of such a thing.

It also came to our attention that Alamo has had a few issues concerning being left alone; she hates it. For instance, Alamo has destroyed two expensive overstuffed couches that Ed had to haul off to the dump. And, more recently, it was discovered that Alamo has some hidden musical talents—she loves piano stools and has eaten the legs and corners off of two of them. Wendi told me that they now use a chair from the kitchen to sit on when playing their piano.

In June 2005, when I spoke to Wendi again, she told me during our conversation that she and Ed had changed Alamo's name to Ala-No! After a lot of laughing and catching up on Alamo's latest fiascos, she told me that Alamo was the best dog that they had ever had, and she thanked us again for picking her out for them.

Then, in a hushed voice, Wendi went on to tell me that Ed's mother had lung cancer and emphysema and had moved in with them. Wendi said that her mother-in-law was insanely in love with Alamo even though every morning Alamo rushes into her bedroom and wakes her up by jumping on top of her and showering her with kisses! On top of all of that, Alamo also keeps a close eye on Ed's mother and stays beside her during the day keeping her company. In Wendi's words, "Alamo is a godsend." Before ending our conversation Wendi told me that it was so sweet to watch her mother-in-law and Alamo enjoy each other and Alamo's official new job title is "caregiver."

Oh! Domino!

On November 30, 1998, Tony and I were home watching a Monday Night Football game on television. It was just a few minutes before halftime, when we heard a horn honking. It was dark outside, but we saw a vehicle with its lights on parked in front of our gate. Tony threw on a jacket and drove down to see who it was.

He found an older man, extremely drunk, leaning on our gate for support. The man told Tony that he had driven all of the way down from San Marcos, to bring us his sorry dog, Cujo.

Tony told the man that he should have called us first before driving down, because we would have told him not to come, because our pens were full and there was no room for Cujo.

The man got angry and began loudly cussing Tony out. I could hear him from our trailer. I threw on my jacket and began walking down to the gate to see what in the world was going on.

When I got to the gate, the man straightened up and quit cussing. He began crying in his beer can instead. He told me in a slurred voice that he loved all dogs, especially his two Pit Bulls, but not Cujo. He told us that Cujo hated all men and that was why he wanted to dump him on us.

With every word that this man slurred, Tony and I grew angrier. This man was drunker than a skunk, and full of B.S.! He kept talking about how much he loved his dog Cujo but would then threaten to throw Cujo off a bridge if we didn't take him. Little did this guy know that Tony was already thinking about throwing him off a bridge.

After hearing this drunk repeat himself over and over again for over forty minutes, Tony opened our gate and told the man to follow us up to our trailer—we would take Cujo.

The whole time that this had been going on, Cujo quietly sat in his crate in the back of this man's pickup. When it was time for us to get Cujo out of his crate, this cockeyed man warned Tony to let me do it, because Cujo would try to kill Tony!

I cautiously opened the door of Cujo's crate and looked inside. I saw one of the sweetest faces that I had ever seen looking back at me. He was a black-and-white spotted medium-sized Cocker/Pointer mix with beautiful brown eyes. I told Cujo that everything was going to be all right and then hooked a leash to his collar. Cujo slowly came out of his cage and jumped down to the ground, and I took him for a short walk before putting him in a pen with Easy, a gentle, male black Labrador.

When I went back up to the pickup, I told the man not to ever come back to the rescue ranch, and to get off of Tony's and my land immediately, or else I would call the sheriff!

In my entire life, I have never said anything like that to anyone, and after I had said it, I was shocked at myself for being so bold. I must have scared the heck out of this creep, because he jumped inside his pickup and drove off. As soon as he was gone, Tony drove down to the gate and closed it.

The following morning, I went outside to check on Cujo, and, before I arrived at his and Easy's pen, I made a decision that Cujo was going to get a new name, no matter how mean of a dog he was. After about ten minutes of petting and playing with the dogs I realized that there was nothing wrong with Cujo at all. I asked Tony, who had been watching us from a distance, to come join me in the pen.

Once Tony was inside Easy's and Cujo's pen, Easy ran to Tony to greet him, and Cujo followed his lead. When Tony reached down to pet Cujo, he jumped up on Tony's leg, with tail wagging, and licked Tony's hand! Cujo didn't hate men—he just hated his previous owner. We were so relieved.

I called Kinky to tell him about the night before, and about Cujo. Before I could finish my story, Kinky had already advised me to change Cujo's name and was delighted to hear that he was a great dog, and not a mean one. Kinky also could not believe what I had said to Cujo's former owner and was proud of me.

Later that afternoon, Jo West came out to the rescue ranch for the very first time. While giving her a tour, we told her about the night before and Cujo. We asked her to help us rename him after she had met him.

"Domino!" Jo said. "What do you think?"

Tony and I loved it, so from then on Cujo was now Domino, and

Kinky thought it was an excellent name when he met Domino a few days later.

Easy and Domino had become best friends fast. Even though they were two males it did not seem to matter. A lot of people believe that putting two males together will cause them to fight, but we have found that not to be true. Tony matches up the dogs at the rescue ranch by personality—not gender.

On Tuesday, November 22, 1999, Tony and I were having lunch at the Lost Maples Cafe in Utopia, when Valerie Moore, our waitress and friend, interrupted our lunch to tell us that a man named John wanted to meet us. We didn't have a problem with that, so Valerie waved John over to our table to join us.

Following the introductions John told us that he was in Utopia having lunch with his friends from his Harley Davidson club who were touring the Hill Country. He asked us if we had any Labradors. Together, Tony and I answered yes! We invited John and his friends to come out and visit the rescue ranch after lunch.

After everyone paid their bills, John and his friends followed us out to the rescue ranch. When the dogs heard the "hogs" coming down the road behind us, they went into a major howl. As soon as everyone parked, the dogs immediately hushed.

After giving a tour to them, John told us that he wanted to adopt Sara, a young yellow Lab, and Fred and Eileen told us they wanted to adopt Domino! Since they were on their Harleys, it was agreed that they would come back in two days, on Thanksgiving Day, to pick up their dogs.

After John and his friends left, I phoned Kinky to tell him the exciting news. As usual, Kinky was very happy about Sara and Domino getting adopted, but then he got a little depressed; he didn't want them to leave the ranch because he would miss them. After reassuring Kinky that the dogs were going to super homes, he was happy again.

Tony and I then went outside to tell Sara and Domino their good news. They acted as if they already knew. Sara was excited about getting a new collar and even tried to help Tony slip it on her.

Domino's reaction to getting a new collar was just the opposite. Even though Domino was jumping up and down and seemed overly happy, he did not want to have anything to do with the collar. Every time that Tony tried to put the collar around Domino's neck, he would back off and act scared.

Tony and I were upset about Domino, because we knew that this was finally his chance to go live a happy life, and if he would not let us put a collar on him, Fred and Eileen might change their minds and decide to adopt one of our other dogs. I called Kinky to tell him about Domino's problem. He told me to call our friend Copper Love, who is an expert when it comes to dealing with problem animals. Copper, besides being an extremely talented plein air artist, is also a Senior Instructor for the TTEAM-TTouch, developed by Linda Tellington-Jones, which heals the body and retrains horses and dogs in a gentle holistic manner. (For more information about Copper, go to www.copperlove.com.)

I called Copper and told her about Domino and that we needed her help immediately. Unfortunately, she told me that she was booked, and Saturday morning would be the earliest she could get out to the ranch.

On Thanksgiving morning, John and Fred arrived, ready to pick up their dogs. I hated having to tell Fred about Domino, but he told me not to worry and to take as much time as was needed—he and Eileen definitely wanted him.

It was now time to adopt Sara. While Tony went to get her, John signed off on the adoption papers, and she was ready to go. She was one happy dog!

After saying our good-byes, Tony and I watched as John and Fred left the rescue ranch with one happy yellow Lab bouncing up and down in their back seat. After they left I phoned Kinky to update him. We agreed that this was the best Thanksgiving Day that the three of us had had in a long time.

On Saturday morning, Copper arrived at the rescue ranch. She was armed with a green harness, sliced up hot dogs, and her "magic blue scarf"—she was ready to go to work! She asked Tony to help her to keep the dogs calm in the pen.

After sitting down in the pen, Copper pulled out her "magic blue scarf" and began feeding Easy and Domino treats, with the scarf in her hand, while talking softly to them. Domino hesitated a few times but then started taking the treats as easy as Easy. The dogs ate it up! A few minutes later, while still giving treats, she began slowly moving the scarf across their shoulders and around their bodies. The dogs didn't seem to care as long as Copper continued to feed them the hot dogs. This went on for about five minutes, and then Copper said it was time to take a break. She and Tony left the pen.

After a fifteen-minute break, it was time for Tony and Copper to get back to work. She told Tony that this time, instead of using her "magic blue scarf," she would be using the green harness, which hopefully they would be able to get on Domino. When Tony and Copper returned to the pen, the dogs could not wait to get back to work. She did the same thing with the green harness and Domino hesitated again, but his love for the hot dogs was stronger than his fear of the harness. He quickly forgot about the harness, and, in less than a couple of minutes, Copper had Domino putting his head in and out of the harness to get more treats!

It was time to put the harness on Domino. When Copper gave Tony a signal, he gently hooked up the harness as Copper talked to Domino and praised him. When the leash was attached to the harness, Tony and Copper led Domino out of the pen. He more or less pranced as he walked between Copper and Tony. We each took turns walking Domino around the ranch while praising him for being so brave and continuing to give him treats. Domino was having a blast!

When Copper returned Domino to his pen, she removed the harness and whispered to him before leaving his pen. Domino hated seeing his new friend leave him and barked until she was out of his sight. Copper told us that she wanted to be here when we adopted Domino, so that she could help with the harness. We told her we would call her when we found out the time.

Domino howled as Copper drove away.

Once she was gone, I phoned Fred and Eileen to tell them that Domino was now ready to be adopted. Fred told me they would be at the rescue ranch tomorrow at high noon! That evening I phoned Copper to thank her and to tell her Domino's adoption would be at noon on Sunday. Then I called Kinky with the exciting news.

On Sunday, Copper, Eileen, and Fred arrived at the rescue ranch. After introductions Copper explained how to put the harness on and guaranteed them that in no time flat, Domino would look forward to putting on his green harness.

We went to the pen and watched Copper work with Domino for a few minutes before Tony hooked up the harness and attached a leash. Domino was excited and led Copper out of the pen to go for a walk. Fred and Eileen took turns walking and praising him, as he proudly strutted back and forth in front of us.

While Fred walked Domino, Eileen filled out our adoption form and signed it. It was official; Domino was now adopted!

Copper, Tony, and I teared up when it was time for Fred, Eileen, and Domino to leave. As they drove away, the three of us saw Domino, who was in the back seat of their truck, turn his head and look back at us.

Copper's and my tear gates opened up, and Tony walked off, wiping something from his eye.

The Boomerang Dogs

On Friday afternoon, January 15, 1999, a woman showed up at the rescue ranch in Utopia to dump off two puppies that she had found criss-crossing the Leakey highway. She was certain that they would have been hit by a car and killed if she had not stopped and picked them up. Her problem was that she could not keep the puppies, and we were her last resort. She told Tony that if we didn't take them she was headed to the pound. We took them.

When Tony went to unload the puppies from a cage in the back of her station wagon, his jaw dropped and so did mine when we saw them—they were huge!

The puppies looked to be about three months old. They definitely had German Shepherd in them, mixed with something gigantic from another planet. Tony and I had never seen such giant puppies in our lives. They weighed over forty pounds each and still had their puppy teeth! Their coats were black and tan, just like a German Shepherd's, but they each had a little patch of white on them, too.

While Tony carried the elephantine male puppy to his pen, I named him Big Foot, because his paws were bigger than the delicious pancakes served at the famous Lost Maples Cafe in Utopia. When Tony returned to the station wagon to get Big Foot's sister, he told me that his back had just gone out on him and he was in pain.

I didn't want to sacrifice my back to the cause, so I grabbed a leash and a collar from our pickup so we could walk Big Foot's sister to his pen. The female puppy's head was so large we couldn't get the collar to slip over her head. Instead, we had to make a noose out of the leash to take her to her pen. When we released her in her new pen to join her brother, I named her Kate, in honor of my mother.

Three days later, Kate and Big Foot were spayed and neutered, wormed, vaccinated, and given a clean bill of health.

Kinky was out of town at this time, and, after I described the pair of puppies to him, he couldn't wait to see and meet them. A week later, when he met Kate and Big Foot, he was as astonished by their size as were Tony and I—they had each gained over ten pounds and had grown two inches taller! Of course, Kinky fell in love with our two loveable giants, and, before leaving the ranch that day, he told us that he was going to make some phone calls to try to get them adopted.

Unfortunately, Kinky's mission to find homes for Kate and Big Foot failed; nobody wanted the gargantuan pups—they were too big!

Finally, a brave little couple from Sabinal (they were each no taller than five feet) came to the rescue ranch and adopted Kate on March 1, 1999. That adoption lasted for one solid week.

The tiny couple returned Kate to us, because when they took her home, she turned into a completely different dog than she had been at our rescue ranch. They said Kate refused to eat or play with their small children and seemed depressed.

When the "munchkins from Sabinal" helped Tony return Kate to her pen they were stupefied, because she instantly turned back into a happy, playful pup when she saw her brother, Big Foot. As we watched Big Foot and Kate run to each other and begin licking, kissing, and sniffing each other happily, the little people swore to us that Kate's happy nature was completely opposite of the way that she had behaved at their home, and they didn't understand why Kate preferred Big Foot to them. In a short amount of time, they left our rescue ranch in a little snit.

About a week later, a man and his wife, also from Sabinal, adopted Big Foot. The following morning, the couple called and told us that Big Foot was gone! He had jumped out of their backyard. They told Tony that they would do everything that they could to find him and would call us immediately if they found him.

Luckily, Big Foot was wearing our identification tags, so I stayed inside the trailer for most of the day, hoping to receive a phone call from someone who had found him. I knew he would be hard to miss, since he was most likely the biggest dog in Sabinal. All day long the phone rang. Besides Kinky calling me every hour to see if Big Foot had been found, the call that I was hoping for never came.

When it was dark, Tony told me that he was going to Sabinal, which is approximately twenty-two miles away, to find Big Foot. I stayed near the phone. In less that twenty minutes, the dogs outside began barking. I went to the window and saw a vehicle driving up to the trailer. I went outside and was shocked to see it was Tony. Why had he come back? When Tony saw me he honked the horn and flashed the lights of the pickup as he drove up to park. "I found Big Foot!" he yelled. "I found him walking down the highway about five miles out of Utopia!"

While Tony returned Big Foot to his pen, I called the couple in Sabinal to let them know that Tony had found Big Foot! The couple was relieved to hear my news, but after the good news came the bad news— they didn't want him back.

I phoned Kinky and told him that Tony had found Big Foot on the highway to Sabinal and reassured him that Big Foot was fine and back with Kate. Kinky was delighted to hear the good news about Big Foot, but he was extremely upset with Big Foot's adopters and blamed them for Big Foot's escape. He told me that he didn't want us to take Big Foot back to those people, because they didn't deserve to have him. I agreed with Kinky about the adopters' negligence with Big Foot, and then told him that it wasn't a problem anyway. The adopters didn't want Big Foot back.

The next day, Kinky phoned to ask us to join him for lunch, later in the afternoon, in Kerrville, to discuss Kate and Big Foot. We did. While we ate Mexican food at the Acapulco Restaurant, it was decided that from here on out, Kate and Big Foot could only be adopted out together, because they loved each other so much. The three of us made a pact, over dessert, that none of us would ever separate them again.

Kinky paid for our lunch, and then we went outside the restaurant and visited for a few minutes in the parking lot, discussing some of our other dogs, while Kinky puffed steadily on his lit cigar, thinking up ways on what he could do to get more adoptions for the rescue ranch. With enough said, Tony and I returned to Utopia, and Kinky departed for Echo Hill Ranch.

On September 26, 1999, a very nice couple drove out to the rescue ranch from Dripping Springs to possibly adopt one of our dogs for their one-hundred-acre ranch. Claire and Jack were two of the nicest people that we had met in a long time. Tony and I knew that whatever dog that they picked out would be well taken care of.

After we gave them a tour of the rescue ranch, Jack and Claire told us they wanted to adopt Kate and Big Foot! This was great news. When I went inside to do the adoption paperwork, I called Kinky.

Kinky was very excited to hear my news, and then, as always, he began interrogating me about who these people were, etc. After telling him everything that I knew about Jack and Claire, it finally dawned on him that he knew and also liked them. Case closed. Ten minutes later, Kate and Big Foot left our ranch in a big, fancy Suburban.

From time to time, Claire would call the ranch to give us updates on the dynamic duo. Claire told me that they had sent Kate and Big Foot to an expensive obedience school, but each had flunked out because Kate and Big Foot wouldn't pay attention—they were preoccupied with each other. She told me that they also were concerned with them because Kate and her brother seemed happy just to be together and really didn't seem to care about interacting with her or Jack.

In the last call we received from Claire, six months later, she told us they were going to have to return Kate and Big Foot to the rescue ranch. They felt horrible about having to return the dogs, but it just hadn't worked out for several reasons.

The straw that broke the camel's back was that Jack had hurt his back trying to lift them into their Suburban because they would not load up, and every time that they needed to take Kate and Big Foot somewhere, Jack would have to pick them up and put them into their vehicle.

We fully understood their problem—especially Tony.

When Kate and Big Foot came back to the rescue ranch they quickly settled into their old digs and seemed happy enough. Time marched on. Every time someone came to the rescue ranch, Kate and Big Foot would sadly be passed over because of their humongous size.

After we had moved the rescue ranch over to Echo Hill, Kate got hurt. We had only been at Echo Hill Ranch for three months when Tony went out in the morning to feed and clean the dog pens. He was in the barn filling the buckets with dog food when Kate rushed inside in a bloody mess!

One side of her muzzle was basically gone, with dangling strips of torn skin flapping. Even though her tail was wagging, she needed emergency help. Tony rushed to the trailer, his hands covered in blood, and told me to call Dr. Craig Janssen at Hoegemeyer Animal Clinic and tell him, "We have an emergency and are coming in now! Kate got into a fight with a wild hog!"

As I made the phone call, Tony rushed Kate to Kerrville.

I then called Kinky to tell him about Kate. He was very concerned and asked me to please update him when I had more news. Tony called me about forty-five minutes later to inform me that Kate was going to be fine, but she needed to have the side of her face sewn up. Craig wanted to keep her at the clinic for at least a week, so he could keep a close eye on her. Tony also told me to stay inside the trailer and not to go outside, because there was a huge wild hog—dead—near Kate's and Big Foot's pen, and he didn't want me to see it. Tony then told me that Kate must have jumped over the five-foot fence and gotten into a big fight with the wild hog, and, obviously, neither had won the battle.

After hanging up, I immediately phoned Kinky to tell him about Kate and the wild hog.

"I already know," Kinky said. "I just got off of the phone with Dr. Janssen. I had called him to talk to Tony, but Tony was on the cell phone talking to you, so Craig filled me in on the details. Don't worry, Kate's going to be fine."

When Tony arrived back at the rescue ranch, he buried the hog and then came to the trailer, and thank goodness he no longer had blood all over his hands.

It was a very long week for Big Foot. We could tell that he was worried about his sister, because he quit eating and seemed despondent. No matter what we tried, we could not get him to wag his tail or eat. We took turns daily going to his pen and talking to him, trying to comfort him. Nothing worked.

Big Foot's tail finally wagged when Tony returned Kate to her pen. The side of her muzzle looked pretty ugly, but, in time, she healed and the fur grew back. In fact, after six months or so, you couldn't even see the scars. She looked perfectly fine.

On the morning of May 30, 2004, Tony found that Kate and Big Foot had been porcupined. Their heads were covered with hundreds of toothpick-like quills. Fortunately, there was no dead porcupine—it must have gotten away. Kate and Big Foot must have tried to get it through the fence, but all they got was a quick ride to Kerrville to see Dr. Janssen to get their quills removed. They had to be anesthetized because it is a painful procedure. Craig told us that he spent over an hour removing the quills from inside their mouths, and from their head, feet, and chest areas.

Monday morning, at 7:10, I called KRVL 94.3 to do the "Steve & Harley Show" and talk about the rescue ranch. When I told them about Kate and Big Foot having been porcupined, they started teasing me about our two jumbo dogs. It was a hilarious show and I could not quit laughing.

Following the "Steve & Harley Show," a young woman named Colleen called and asked me if she could adopt them. My answer was yes, but my question was, did you listen to the "Steve & Harley Show" this morning? Colleen told me that she had heard the show but told me that she had already fallen in love with them before this morning.

"How could this be?" I wondered. Colleen had never been out to the rescue ranch, so I asked her. Come to find out, she had just started working at Hoegemeyer Animal Clinic, and when Tony showed up with the terrific twosome, she was the one who helped remove their quills.

On Saturday morning, June 12, 2004, Colleen arrived at the ranch with her sister and adopted Kate and Big Foot. After signing the adoption forms, Kate and Big Foot happily loaded up in her car and were ready to go live on Colleen's big ranch near Kerrville.

On several occasions we ran into Colleen at Hoegemeyer Animal Clinic, and she would fill us in on their antics. She told us that Kate and Big Foot were sleeping inside at night and roaming the range during the day, and they seemed to be very happy at their new home. Knowing that Kate and Big Foot were doing so well made Kinky, Tony, and me extremely happy. That lasted for three weeks.

On July 3, 2004, Kate and Big Foot were returned to us, again. Colleen was heartbroken about it. Her neighbors had accused Kate and Big Foot of killing one of their goats and had threatened to shoot them if they ever caught them on their ranch again. Kinky, Tony, and I were all disappointed when Kate and Big Foot returned—but not Kate and her brother! Once out of Colleen's car they happily dragged Kinky and Tony back to their spacious pen to take up residence.

After I told Steve and Harley about Kate and Big Foot being returned to us for maybe killing a goat, they would ask me, every Monday morning, from then on, to give them an update about the latest escapades of Kate and Big Foot. Thanks to the "Steve & Harley Show," Kate and Big Foot became famous in the Hill Country and throughout Central Texas. If Kinky, Tony, or I were in Kerrville, we would often be stopped by people asking us about Kate and Big Foot. Some people even drove out to the rescue ranch just to meet them and to have their pictures taken with them! And, no—they did not have to use a wide-angle lens.

On Saturday, December 19, 2004, our rescue ranch received one of the best phone calls that we have ever received. Robert McGee, from Harlingen, Texas, had seen Kate and Big Foot's pictures up on our website, and he wanted to know if they were mean dogs. He told me that he and his wife, Evelyn, did not want mean dogs—they just wanted a couple of dogs that would have a "presence" on their ranch, to keep strangers from trespassing.

I told Robert that Kate and Big Foot were definitely not vicious dogs and guaranteed him that no one would dare think about trespassing on their property once they had laid their eyes on Kate and her bigger brother.

That was exactly what Robert and Evelyn were looking for. Kate and Big Foot were adopted on Sunday morning, December 19, 2004, to one super family. Robert, Evelyn, and their son, Scott, had gotten up at the crack of dawn to make the five-hour drive to adopt Kate and Big Foot. They arrived at the rescue ranch about ten-thirty in the morning and fell in love with Kate and Big Foot by ten-thirty-one! It took Kate and

Big Foot less than one minute to fall in love with them, too, and we were totally impressed with Robert, Evelyn, and Scott.

After signing the adoption papers and making a very generous donation to the rescue ranch, it was time for them to leave. Kate and Big Foot loaded up easily into the back of their Suburban, and, before they could close the door, Scott jumped into the back to ride the long drive back with Kate and Big Foot. Once again, Kinky, Tony, and I, were ecstatic with joy about Kate and her brother getting a super home—once again!

Later that Sunday evening, Evelyn called to tell us that Kate and Big Foot were fabulous dogs, and that she and her family could not thank us enough for letting them adopt them.

When I phoned Kinky to tell him the great news about Kate and Big Foot, he said, "I can't believe it, Nance. I had just about given up on those two ever finding a home, and then out of nowhere, good people show up like Robert and his family. I hope it sticks!"

So far, so good—it has stuck! As I write this on July 5, 2005, it has been over six months since Kate and her sidekick, Big Foot, left our rescue ranch.

To date, whenever I am describing a big dog to Steve and Harley, they always ask me, "Is the dog as big as Kate and Big Foot?"

Her Name Is Barbra

In my wildest dreams, I never would have thought that I would end up meeting Barbra Streisand hiding under a dumpster at the Sabinal city dump!

On Saturday, August 25, 2001, I had to go to Sabinal, Texas, twenty-some miles from Utopia, to dispose of our weekly supply of dog poop. The man in charge of the dump told me that a little dog was hiding under one of the dumpsters, and he was afraid that it was hurt, because he kept hearing it whimper. He asked me to please try to help him get the dog out from under the dumpster.

We went over to the empty dumpster, and the clearance from it to the ground was only about ten inches. I thought to myself, this must be one tiny dog to be able to get underneath this giant trash bin. I was halfway right.

I got down on my hands and knees and leaned down so I could look under the dumpster. I saw a scared little brown dog about three feet away from me, staring blankly back at me. I tried to reach for her, but she was too far away. As I spoke to her, the employee at the dump went to the building and brought back his lunch in a brown paper sack. He offered it to me to use as bait to help coax her out.

I chose his bologna sandwich as the bait. I tore off a little piece of bread and laid it as close to her as I could get it. She sniffed, crawled to it, and ate it. It was now O-S-C-A-R time. I took a small piece of meat and laid it closer to me. She slowly crawled to it and devoured it. She was now almost within my reach. It took only two more times of bologna-baiting before she crawled out from under the empty bin on her own.

I felt sick and angry when I first saw her in full daylight. She was starved down to nothing and had been shot in the front leg, which was dangling and blackened from gangrene; whoever had beaten her had broken her jaw in several places, but she was still able to wag her tail at us.

The man was scared to touch her so I reached down, picked her up, and carried her to the pickup, and laid her on the front seat. She needed immediate medical attention, so I phoned Tony and asked him what I should do, because I was too far away from Hoegemeyer's and Sabinal didn't have a vet clinic. Tony remembered hearing great things about the vet in Hondo and suggested that I drive her there; it was only twenty-two miles away. He told me that he would call them and alert them that I was on my way, and then call me back to give me the directions to the clinic.

We were five miles outside of Sabinal when Tony phoned me back with the details. I had to drive the last fifteen miles with my windows rolled down because of the horrible stench from her leg. She did great on the ride over to the vet clinic. She just laid there on the front seat nibbling as best she could on the bologna sandwich.

When we arrived at the Hondo Veterinary Hospital, several cars were parked out front for last-minute veterinary care before the office closed at noon. I decided to go inside first and let them know that we had arrived. That was a good decision, because when I walked into the lobby, it was full of kids with their parents waiting patiently to see the doctor.

I went up to the counter and introduced myself, and told the receptionist that the dog was in such bad shape that I would wait out in the truck, so the children would not have to see her—it might scare them. She told me to drive around to the back of the clinic, and she would send one of their vet technicians out to the truck to bring her in the back door.

A nice young woman was standing outside the back door waiting for us when we pulled up. She was horrified when she saw the shape that the dog was in. She carefully picked her up and then asked me to go back to the lobby to wait for Dr. Riff to speak to me after he was finished with his clients.

The wait didn't take long at all. After all of the people had cleared the lobby, a very nice man came out the door and introduced himself to me as Dr. Glen Riff. He told me that he had just looked at the dog. Her front leg needed to be amputated immediately, and her jaw had been broken in at least three places. He explained to me that because she was so very weak, she might not survive the amputation. In fact, she was in such bad shape, she might not survive at all. He warned me that it was also going to be fairly expensive and asked me what I wanted him to do; because she was in a lot of pain, a decision had to be made immediately.

I told him to do whatever he could to save her.

He told me that he would stay after hours and amputate her leg immediately, and while she was still under he would wire her jaw back together. He told me that he would call me on Monday to tell me how it went, and then he went to prep for her surgery.

As I turned to leave, the receptionist asked me to wait so I could give her some information. After giving her the information about the rescue ranch, her final question was, "Does the dog have a name?"

"Yes," I answered. "Her name is Barbra—Barbra Streisand."

Monday morning, I called the Hondo Veterinary Hospital to check on Barbra. Dr. Riff told me that she had survived the amputation, but she was not out of the woods yet. It would be touch and go for a few more days to see if she would survive.

On Thursday morning, August 30, 2001, Dr. Riff called to tell us that we could come and pick up Barbra and bring her to the rescue ranch. As soon as we heard the good news, Maribeth and I took off for the Hondo Veterinary Hospital. When we arrived at the hospital, Dr. Riff came out to the lobby and told us that Barbra was definitely a survivor. He said that during the surgery he had almost lost her twice because she was so weak. He was also amazed by her fast recovery and that she had gained over six pounds since her amputation! He recommended that we give her plenty of tender, loving care, feed her gruel, and for us to give her a pen all to herself, until her wound was completely healed. He also wanted us to bring Barbra back to his hospital in a week to check on her jaw. The last thing Dr. Riff did was to apologize for having to charge us so much, but he did mention that he had given us a little discount before leaving his lobby.

Talk about a discount! I nearly did a flip in the lobby when his receptionist presented me with Barbra's bill. I was expecting it to be at least a thousand dollars and praying that it would be no more than fifteen hundred. Before I filled out the check, I asked the receptionist if she was sure about the amount, and she said yes while wearing a great, big smile.

The check that I wrote the Hondo Veterinary Hospital was for two hundred and eighty-six dollars and sixty cents! I could not believe how generous Dr. Riff had been to us. The medicine alone definitely cost over a hundred dollars.

After I paid the bill, it was now showtime. Barbra came hopping out on her three legs and was happily wagging her tail at us. She looked great!

"Look!" Maribeth remarked. "I think she's smiling at us!"

When the three of us arrived back at the rescue ranch, Tony and I decided to give Barbra the use of my writing cabin because it was much nicer than a pen. Barbra seemed to love her new digs, because when she went inside, she immediately jumped up on my couch and sat down.

Tony, Maribeth, and I could not get over how happy she seemed after all that she had been through.

Nick Marsh, one of our good friends in Utopia and a volunteer for the rescue ranch, showed up and immediately fell in love with her. He told us before leaving that he wanted to adopt Barbra, after she was fully recovered, for his mother who lived up in Fort Worth.

On September 5, 2001, Tony and I took Barbra to see Dr. Riff. After a full examination, he recommended that we should take Barbra up to Austin to see an orthopedic surgeon about her jaw and then gave Barbra a rabies shot. The soonest that the orthopedic surgeon up in Austin could see her was Thursday, September 13. That morning, Maribeth and I drove Barbra up to Austin for her appointment. After the doctor examined her, she told us that Barbra's jaw was going to be fine, and she did not recommend surgery.

On October 30, Barbra had fully recovered, and Nick Marsh came over to the rescue ranch and adopted her for his mother. Tony and I were a little sad to let her go, but Nick promised us that she would have a great home and be well taken care of. And, before Nick drove off with Barbra Streisand happily sitting on the front seat of his pickup, he told us that we would see Barbra often, because he had promised his mother that he would babysit Barbra anytime that she needed to be out of town.

Recently, when we spoke to Nick, he told us that Barbra was doing great, and he had just babysat her for the weekend. He told us that when his mother came to pick Barbra up, she could not wait to jump into his mother's car to resume sharing the comfortable lifestyle with his mother.

"Barbra Streisand is spoiled rotten," Nick told us. "She's turned into a diva!"

Pretty Mama

In the middle of May 2002, the rescue ranch received an urgent call from an extremely distressed woman living in the Hill Country. I took the call, and while this poor woman sobbed into the telephone, I began to cry, too.

Between fits of crying, the elderly woman begged me to take her dog. She told me that her beloved husband of forty-something years of marriage had just died two days earlier of a heart attack, and she was beside herself as to what to do about his six-month-old puppy. Her caring children wanted to take her away for a few months, and she didn't want to board the dog, because she didn't want to keep it, because every time that she looked at it, it made her think of her dear husband and would make her cry. She then told me that her neighbor had offered to shoot the dog—and her children had offered to take it to the veterinarian to be euthanized—but she wouldn't have any of that.

Not knowing anything about this puppy, I told the woman that we would take it. That made her cry worse. Finally, after the woman had regained her composure, we decided to meet in Kerrville later that day to deliver and pick up the dog.

When I arrived in Kerrville at the designated parking lot, the woman was already waiting for me with the dog standing in the back of her pickup. The minute I saw the dog, I got goose bumps and tears welled up in my eyes—it was a Great Pyrenees!

There were two reasons why seeing the dog had upset me.

For the past few months, I had found myself being somewhat depressed and wishing that my parents were still around so I could talk to them. In fact, they had both appeared in my dreams a couple of times in the previous week, and I had remembered talking to them about wanting another Great Pyrenees and had even asked them to help me find one. The only thing else that I remember about those dreams was them telling me they loved me.

Now the reason that I had been thinking about getting another Great Pyrenees was because during my entire adult life I had always had at least one Great Pyrenees living with me, but it had now been over seven years since I last had one.

Before I got out of the truck to greet the little old woman, I said a little silent prayer of thanks. As soon as I got out of the truck, the woman rushed over to me and hugged me tight. After letting go of me, she thanked me over and over again for our rescue ranch helping her and the dog.

Before introducing me to the dog, she handed me the dog's veterinarian records, and then she began crying. Cars were slowing down as they passed by us standing there in the middle of the parking lot, with her crying and me trying to console her.

After she had settled down, it was time to meet her late husband's dog. She cautioned me to stand back a few feet as she lowered the tailgate of her pickup and took hold of the dog's leash. I questioningly heeded her advice and backed off.

Before I knew what was happening, the woman dropped the leash and the giant pup then leaped out of the back end of the truck and ran straight to me! Then it jumped up and began hugging my shoulders, and kissing me on the face. Before the widow could apologize, I was laughing while hugging this gentle white giant. The dog loved me, and no Pyrenees had ever been that overly affectionate with me—ever. I was so happy!

After the kisses and hugging subsided, the woman thanked me again for our help, and then climbed up into her truck and drove away. Before I put this loveable dog into the cab of the pickup, I opened up the dog's papers to find out if it was a male or female, even though it didn't really matter to me, because I knew that I was going to adopt this sweet dog anyway. I discovered that the dog was a female, and she was only five months old instead of six, and then a chill went down my spine when I read that she was born on January 19th—my mother's birthday!

Some might call it a coincidence, but I firmly believe that it was a godsend and that my parents had been a part of it, too.

By the time we arrived back at the rescue ranch, she and I were best friends. She had ridden the twenty-something miles sitting right beside me and kissing me on the face the entire trip. Tony knew the minute that he saw us drive up that the dog was going inside our trailer and not to an outside pen as planned. As we got out of the truck, he teased me about being careful what I dreamed for as my dog hugged him and showered him with kisses.

Later that night, my new dog did the weirdest thing that I have ever witnessed a dog do—she copied me.

I was fixin' to go to bed, and she followed me as I went into our bedroom and then into the restroom, because I needed to tinkle before I went to bed. When I sat down on the toilet seat, she walked into our walk-in shower, and, while staring at me, she squatted down and tinkled the same time that I did! I was in shock and wondered who had taught her that trick. And, please note, I flushed and she did not—and she has never to my knowledge done it again.

The next day, when I told Kinky and Tony about her being a godsend, and being born on my mother's birthday, it blew them out of their saddles. And they both laughed about her bathroom skills.

It took me over a week to find the right name for my dog, but thanks to Kinky I finally came up with it. In fact, I stole it from him. Kinky had previously given me a galley copy of his latest book to read, *Meanwhile Back at the Ranch*, a novel about our rescue ranch—which, in my opinion, was one of the best books that he has ever written, and not just because I'm in it.

Anyway, one of the characters in this book was a woman named Hattie Mamajello. When I read her name, it literally caused me to laugh out loud. Then it hit me—Mamajello would be my Pyrenees's name. It said it all! It was perfect.

Tony liked the name, and Kinky was delighted with it. Since then, we have shortened it to Mama.

Also since that time, Mama has ruled our trailer, and when Mama barks—everyone listens. And, to my disappointment—I guess because I thought I was special to her—every person that has ever entered our yard or trailer is greeted by Mama with the same affection that she showed me the first time that we met. And, lastly, she sleeps between us on our bed every night.

The Cat's Meow

Saturday, October 18, 2003, the day after my birthday, I was still celebrating, because one of our favorite people, Jo West, was coming to visit us and we couldn't wait to see her. It had been nearly two years since we last saw Jo, and, besides that, it would be the first time for her to see our new ranch in Medina.

First, here's a little history. Tony and I first met Jo back in 1998, just a few months after we had started the rescue ranch. Kinky was anxious for his friend, Jo, to come see our new rescue ranch, since she was an avid animal lover like us, so he telephoned her and asked her to come out and meet Tony and me, and to take a tour. He guaranteed her that she would enjoy it.

Tony and I will never forget the first time that we met Jo. She came out to the rescue ranch on Tuesday, December 1, 1998, to meet us and to play with our dogs. We were outside working with the dogs when Jo arrived at the rescue ranch. She was driving a brand new, silver Lincoln Continental. When Jo stopped and parked her car, Tony's rescued Blue Heeler, Blue, ran to her car to greet her. At full speed, he jumped up on the hood of the Lincoln and slid into the windshield.

Tony made a few choice comments about his dog as we raced over to Jo's car to remove Blue from the windshield wipers. Thoughts were flying through my head like: were we fixin' to get sued, cussed out, stuck buying a new Lincoln, etc.?

We reached the car at the same time that Jo exited it—laughing. While Tony removed Blue from the car, I started apologizing to Jo. She continued to laugh. After Tony apologized for his dog's poor greeting etiquette, Jo said, "Stop apologizing—it's only a car. Stop worrying about it—it's just a car." Then she bent down and patted Blue on the head, and asked him if he had a headache.

When Jo left the rescue ranch that day, she was covered with dirt and had been scratched, but was still smiling. Since then, we have met most of her lovely family and nothing has ever been said again about Blue's head-on collision.

Fast forward to Saturday, October 18, 2003. Jo arrived around four o'clock. Nothing had changed about her—she looked great and wore a big smile. Tony and I first took her for a tour of the rescue ranch. After the tour, we went inside my writing cabin to catch up on things. During our visit, the dogs began barking and an old, beat-up pickup truck came driving up. Tony went outside to see who it was. While Tony was outside, Willow, an extremely outgoing, beautiful, black-and-white female rescued cat, played with us inside my building. As Willow took turns sitting in Jo's and my lap, I told Willow's story to Jo.

Willow was an emergency cat rescue. We rescued her and her sister, Ada, on Friday, September 26, 2003, when a young woman and her husband showed up at the rescue ranch. The young couple were dressed in military uniforms, and they begged us to please help them out. They explained to us that they were being sent to Iraq in a matter of days, and no one would take their cats. The young woman began crying. Tony and I went outside and had a short discussion as to what we should do. We went back inside my writing cabin and the young woman had stopped crying. When we told the stressed out couple that we would take their cats, the woman and her husband both began to cry tears of happiness.

After having gone through a box of tissue, the couple took the cats out of their crates and introduced us to them. Miss Puss didn't seem to be real impressed with Tony or me after being introduced, and she hightailed it under the couch.

Willow did exactly the opposite. She marched right up to Tony and purred, and then jumped into his lap so he could pet her. When Willow decided that she had given Tony enough attention, she leaped into the air and landed in my lap from across the room—it was now my turn to enjoy her. Willow's social skills were the best that we had ever seen in a cat. She was prim and proper and outgoing, but always a lady at all times.

While all of this was going on the woman handed me Miss Puss's and Willow's paperwork, and then proudly declared that the cats would be adopted quickly since the couple had spent a lot of their last paycheck having them declawed.

Now it was my turn to cry, but I didn't—no tissues left.

Unfortunately, many unknowing people think that declawing a cat is a painless, humane procedure. They think that declawing a cat is simply the pulling out of the cat's fingernails, quickly and painlessly.

Wrong! Wrong! Wrong! It should be a crime and hopefully will be, if Kinky gets to be governor of our great state of Texas in 2006. If he is elected, he has promised to do everything that he can to outlaw the declawing of cats.

I found out what declawing is from one of our veterinarians, Kim Herndon, when I asked her about it seven years ago. She told me to hold my hands out in front of me with my palms facing up. She then pretended to have a knife in her hand and began "amputating" at the first joint of each finger, one by one. Even though she was just pretending, I hurt. Kim had made her point—declawing is amputation—and cruel!

After saying their good-byes to their declawed cats, the young kids dressed up in military attire thanked us and drove away, headed for Iraq. As soon as the soldiers were gone, I told Tony that I wanted to change Miss Puss's name to Ada. Ada was a close friend to Kinky, and her mother, Lottie, had helped raise Kinky, Marcie, and Roger—they were family. So, to honor Ada Beverly, we named Miss Puss Ada.

I called Kinky to let him know about the cats and to ask him to please tell Ada, who was over at the Lodge visiting Kinky, that we had just named a cat in her honor. Ada was so excited about having a cat named after her, she asked Kinky to bring her over to the rescue ranch so she could meet her namesake.

A few minutes later, Kinky and Ada arrived at the rescue ranch to meet the cats. Ada fell in love with Ada, and Kinky, of course, fell in love with both of the cats. We had a nice visit. They stayed for about an hour playing with the cats and then went back to Kinky's Lodge.

On Sunday, September 28, 2003, Kinky had some friends from Austin come down to visit him for the day. Late in the afternoon, when the couple left to go back home, Ada, the cat, went with them. Thanks to Kinky, we had another great adoption!

Fast forward again to Saturday, October 18, 2003. After I was done telling Jo Willow's story, Tony came into my writing cabin to tell me that the woman outside in the old pickup had just told him if we wouldn't take her dog, she would take the dog home and shoot it in the head!

Jo was horrified. I asked her to please excuse me for a few minutes— I needed to go outside to talk to this woman.

Tony and I went to the old pickup, and this horrible, angry woman, who looked like she had been rode hard and put up wet, repeated herself about killing her dog.

I looked at Tony, he nodded his head, yes. We took the dog.

As soon as the woman was gone, I named the dog Boomer, and Tony took him to a pen and fed and watered him. When I returned to my cabin, Jo and I visited for a little bit longer, and then it was time for her to leave. After saying good-bye, Jo left the rescue ranch.

On Wednesday, October 22, 2003, Jo West called to ask if she could adopt Willow. Our answer was a big, fat yes! When I called Kinky to tell him that Jo wanted Willow, he was delighted with my news. Even though Kinky knew that Willow would wind up being one of the luckiest cats in the world, and would live the life of luxury and love, it saddened him that Willow would be leaving because he had fallen in love with her.

Kinky does this every time that we have an adoption. He is joyful about every adoption, but always gets sad when they leave the rescue ranch. He has often teased me about being the one who cries with every adoption, but he is the one, calling the kettle black.

On Tuesday morning, October 28, 2003, I drove up to Georgetown, Texas, to meet Jo West halfway to deliver precious cargo—Willow West!

Fortunately, Jo and I had timed it perfectly, and we had met up within five minutes of each other. Jo was so happy about adopting Willow, she quickly filled out the adoption form and made a sizeable donation to the rescue ranch.

After Jo had departed with Willow in her brand new, fancy Lincoln, I did cry—I'll admit it.

Rumors have found their way back to the rescue ranch that Willow West has changed Jo's life for the better—she was happier now than she had been in a long time. She and Willow have become inseparable. We have also found out from Jo that Willow has become a real social butterfly—every time that someone goes to visit Jo, Willow races to the door to be the first to greet Jo's guests.

The last time that I spoke to Jo, she told me that her friends and family were jealous of her, because they all wanted their cats to be as cool as Willow.

Thank goodness Boomer showed up at the rescue ranch when he did that day, causing me to leave Jo alone in my cabin for just the right amount of time—to fall in love with Willow.

Every Dog Has a Story

Boomer came to the rescue ranch on Saturday, October 18, 2003. An old, angry woman showed up with him and told us that if we did not take her dog, she would go home and put a bullet in his head. We took him and I named him Boomer.

When we rescued Boomer, he was an energetic, big, black, male Rottweiler mix, about four or five months old, and as sweet as he could be. In other words—he was a great dog.

On October 27, 2003, Boomer was adopted to a woman completely opposite of the one who had owned him previously—she was nice. The woman had fallen in love with Boomer instantly when she met him, just like the rest of us had. She adopted Boomer that day and took him to his new home in Tarpley, Texas, where he would live happily ever after on her ranch—so she thought.

Well, Boomer unfortunately was returned to us eight days later, because he was accused of killing a neighbor's goat. The woman was sick about having to return Boomer, but her neighbors had threatened to shoot him if they ever caught him near their goats again. This kind woman didn't want that to happen to Boomer, so she did the next best thing—she had a friend return him to us, because it was too upsetting for her to deal with.

When Boomer arrived back at the rescue ranch, he was glad to see us and could hardly wait to be put back into his old pen. He literally dragged Tony to it.

On Thursday afternoon, January 8, 2004, Dennis Lanning, a very nice man from Los Angeles, California, showed up at our rescue ranch wanting to see our ranch and possibly adopt one of our great dogs. Tony and I gave him a tour.

During the tour, Dennis told us about himself and what kind of dog he was hoping to find. We discovered that one of Dennis's passions was racing mountain bikes. He took his sport seriously, and he had competed in races all over the United States and was fixin' to go down to Mexico to compete. We also learned that if Dennis wasn't racing in some race, he was riding his bike at least ten miles every day.

After our tour, Dennis told us that he had narrowed down his search to two of our dogs. One was Lefty and the other was Boomer. He told us that he was going to be staying in Kerrville for a few days and wanted to know if he could try them out, one at a time; he would take one to spend the night so he could get to know him. Then he would bring that dog back to us the next morning and take the other one for an overnighter to check him out. Of course, Tony and I said yes, but I wanted to take Dennis over to meet Kinky and make sure Kinky wouldn't object to Dennis's idea.

The three of us went over to Kinky's Lodge and had a short visit, because Kinky was in the middle of writing one of his books and his deadline to turn it in was approaching. Kinky liked Dennis and thought Dennis's idea sounded great.

He said to Dennis, "Do it! Even if it doesn't work out, at least Boomer and Lefty will get a little vacation away from here. It'll be good for them."

That evening, we left the Lodge, and before we were back at the rescue ranch, Dennis had decided to try Lefty first.

Tony and I had rescued Lefty and his brother, Pancho, from the Kerrville pound on September 16, 2003. Their markings were identical, except Lefty was black and white, while Pancho was brown and white, though their personalities were opposite. Lefty was shy and Pancho was outgoing. They were wannabe bird dogs and approximately four months old when we rescued them.

When Tony put a leash on Lefty to take him to Dennis, Lefty did not want to go. He cowered, and so Tony had to carry him to Dennis's car. When he was put into the car Lefty trembled and seemed scared to death. We were all pretty concerned about Lefty's behavior, but Dennis felt that once he got used to the car and him, he would settle down.

The next morning, Dennis showed up bright and early. He had bad news. He told us that Lefty was terrified of everything. He said that when he went to take Lefty for a walk around the motel in Kerrville, Lefty was miserable. He was scared to meet passers-by, garbage cans, and bicycles, and refused to take a treat, eat his dinner, etc. Dennis suggested that we might consider taking him to a doggie shrink.

Tony and I were concerned to hear this news and were baffled about Lefty's behavior. We decided that when Tony returned Lefty to his pen to be reunited with his brother, Dennis and I would watch from a distance. The minute Lefty was unleashed, he turned back into his old self. He raced around the pen playing with Pancho. There was no more trembling or cowering. He acted like a normal dog again! We were all dumbfounded.

We had a short visit with Dennis before it was time for him to leave with dog number two—Boomer. Thank goodness Boomer's reaction to going with Dennis was totally opposite of Lefty's. Boomer couldn't wait to get into Dennis's car and leave. Once again, he literally dragged Tony to Dennis's vehicle. When Dennis opened the door, Boomer jumped in before Tony could say "load up." Boomer was so excited about leaving, I half expected him to start the car and take off before Dennis could load up.

The following morning, January 9, 2004, Dennis called wanting to know if he could keep Boomer for one more day! He was almost positive that he wanted to adopt Boomer but wanted to go bike riding with him on some bike trails to see how he did. Dennis went on to tell Tony that Boomer was an incredibly great dog. That evening, Dennis came back out to the rescue ranch and adopted Boomer officially. Dennis was so impressed with Boomer he couldn't quit bragging about him to Kinky, Tony, and me.

As Dennis continued to rave on about Boomer being such a super dog, we three politely listened with delight, because we already knew it.

When it was time for Dennis to leave the rescue ranch we said our good-byes and then watched Dennis and "the greatest dog on earth" drive away. Kinky then made an interesting comment.

"Hey," Kinky said, "when Dennis was bragging about Boomer, Boomer looked like he was smiling at us the entire time. I have never seen a dog do that. Did y'all catch that, or am I going crazy?"

Tony and I laughed.

"Well, I know for a fact that you're crazy," I teased, "but I noticed it, too."

"Kinky," Tony said, "I'll guarantee you that he was smiling. In all of the years that we have been doing this, I've never seen a dog smile like that."

Sunday morning, supposedly Tony's and my day off, Dennis called the rescue ranch at eight-thirty. Tony took the call. Right off, Dennis told Tony that Boomer was a keeper, but there was one problem with Boomer—he vomits every time that he rides in the car. Tony told Dennis to go to Hoegemeyer Animal Clinic and ask them to give Boomer some Dramamine for Boomer's carsickness.

When Tony gave Dennis the directions to Hoegemeyer Animal Clinic, Dennis remarked, "That's great! Where I'm staying is only about two blocks from there. I can walk Boomer over there, instead of having to drive him there in the 'vomit-mobile'!"

Tony hung up the phone laughing.

Dennis made a few more visits out to the rescue ranch. On his and Boomer's last visit, Dennis told us that Boomer was no longer vomiting, and he had gotten a health certificate on Boomer from Hoegemeyer Animal Clinic, so he could take him into Mexico for a mountain bike race.

From time to time, Dennis e-mailed us with pictures of Boomer's travels and included updates on his super dog. Little did we know that Boomer's story wasn't over yet!

In early May, Kerri Manus, a young woman from California, called the rescue ranch to tell us that she had just met a man named Dennis and his incredible dog, Boomer, at a bike shop in Los Angeles. She told us that she was drawn to Boomer because he was wearing our Texas-shaped dog tags, and also because of the way Boomer kept staring at her as he waited outside the bicycle shop for Dennis's return. She said that

Boomer wouldn't quit smiling at her, and she had never seen anything like it. She decided to wait outside the bike shop to find out more about this fascinating, smiling dog.

When Dennis returned, she introduced herself and then asked Dennis about Boomer. Dennis told her about our rescue ranch and then took the opportunity to brag a little about his wonderful dog. Kerri immediately went home, got on the Internet, and looked us up, and that was why she was calling—to see if she and her friend, Daisy Lynn Mertzel, could drive out on the Memorial Day Weekend to adopt a dog. Our answer was yes!

"I want Uncle Sam!" were the exact words Kerri spoke when she first met Uncle Sam, a wannabe Golden Retriever, on Saturday, May 29, 2004, Memorial Day Weekend at the rescue ranch. It was love at first sight for both of them.

Kerri and Daisy had arrived at the rescue ranch about four o'clock in the afternoon with their dogs. Daisy's dog was a precious little black dog named Percy, and Kerri's dog, Max, was a service dog who she felt needed a companion.

After Kerri had chosen Uncle Sam, we went to my writing cabin to see if the dogs would get along. With all three of their tails wagging, the dogs went into "the getting to know you" sniffing ritual that all dogs do when meeting a new dog. The ritual lasted for about two minutes and Uncle Sam had passed the test.

Everything was fine until Daisy's little dog, Percy, became jealous and had to be excused from the cabin to do a "time out" for five minutes. When he returned from his "time-out corner" he behaved beautifully, even though he did seem a bit embarrassed. After all of the excitement, the dogs settled down and took a nap while Kinky, Tony, and I visited with Daisy and Kerri. Later, when Daisy and Kerri left our rescue ranch, there were three very happy tail-wagging passengers in the back seat headed home to California.

On February 21, 2005, Boomer and Dennis came to the rescue ranch for a visit, and for Kinky, Tony, and I to meet his girlfriend, Marilyn Anderson, the author of *Never Kiss a Frog*. It was an enjoyable time for everyone. Dennis, of course, did brag about Boomer's latest episodes, but on this visit he did a lot more bragging on Marilyn, even though it wasn't necessary—she was great.

If it hadn't been for Boomer being at the right place at the right times, I wonder if Willow, the cat, or Uncle Sam would have found such great homes. And I am sure that Boomer's story is going to be an ongoing saga; I think if Dennis has his way, the story of Boomer, the smiling dog, will become legend.

And that is why I believe Boomer smiles.

On July 2, 2005, I received an e-mail from Dennis, giving me permission to use his and Boomer's real names in this book. Unaware of what I had written about the two of them, Dennis wrote in his e-mail:

"Speaking of The Boomer, guess who else is writing a book? That's right—he is! It's titled *The Boomer—My Life So Far . . . as a Dog*. He's been working on it for a while now, and I hope it will be finished by the end of this summer."

And that is what makes Kinky, Tony, and me smile.

Old Friends

On November 21, 2003, an elderly man called Kinky to ask him if he could please help him out with his dog. The man was being forced to give up his three-and-half-year-old black Labrador Retriever, Tipper—the love of his life.

While crying over the phone, the man explained to Kinky how special his dog was to him and what a great dog Tipper was, but he wouldn't divulge to Kinky why he had to give up his dog.

With the man weeping on the other end of the line, and begging Kinky to please take his dog, Kinky responded in true form—if someone or an animal needed helping, no matter what the circumstances, Kinky would, as always, come to their rescue and help them out if he could. Kinky told the sobbing man to bring his dog to the rescue ranch and not to worry anymore about his dog. Tipper would be just fine.

The one thing that you will never hear from Kinky's lips is that he has spent much of his life rescuing people and animals. I know this for a fact because I am one of his rescues. All of his close friends and family know about Kinky's kindness, but Kinky tries to keep it a secret. But every once in a while, the information leaks out. This character trait or flaw, as he likes to call it, is one of the reasons that he is so dear to my heart. To know Kinky is to love him.

Kinky called to tell us that he was coming over and needed to talk to us. Five minutes later, he was here at the rescue ranch telling Tony and me about this poor old man and his dog. We already knew the story before Kinky began it. Unfortunately, we get at least ten calls a day from all over the country with people begging, crying, and sometimes even trying to bribe us to please take their pets. Saying no to these desperate people is very hard for us to do, but we have to, because if we said yes to everyone who called we could have over 10,000 dogs in a matter of months, all running wild and with no quality of life. We don't consider that rescuing.

Our rescue ranch is set up to take care of fifty dogs and those numbers do vary from time to time. And when Kinky, Tony, and I decided to start the rescue ranch we made a pact from the very beginning that we would not "warehouse" dogs.

Our policy at the rescue ranch is to rescue dogs and cats only from the pound, but from time to time, we do make exceptions, and this time it was Tipper.

Tony told Kinky that the pens were full, and the only place that we could put Tipper would be in one of our big alleys between pens until one of our dogs got adopted. Then we could move Tipper into a pen to share with another dog. With the meeting finished, Kinky drove back over to his Lodge and phoned the elderly man to set up a time for him to bring Tipper to us.

On November 23, 2003, a friend of the family drove the old man and Tipper to our rescue ranch. Kinky, Tony, and I visited with him for about twenty minutes as he shared many pictures that he had taken of Tipper. We saw Tipper swimming in a creek, sitting on a couch, dressed up in holiday costumes, meeting a deer, etc. Kinky stayed for a few more minutes but had to leave because he had an important phone interview to do.

When it was time for the old man to leave he began crying as he helped Tony put Tipper into the alley. Tipper knew exactly what was going on and was very upset. The old man kissed Tipper for one last time, and then he had to be helped back to the truck because he was so shaken.

As the pickup drove away, I started to cry, because I knew that two hearts had just been broken and mine was hurting, too.

Tipper began howling and tried repeatedly to jump over the five-foot fence. Tony and I went to get him some treats in hopes that it would help calm him down. It didn't work.

When we approached Tipper's alley he quit the howling and began growling at us with his teeth barred—like he wanted to kill us. The hair on his back was standing up and he meant business. I think he was blaming us for not letting him leave with his best friend.

When Tony tried to give him a hot dog as a peace offering, he lunged at the gate ready to eat Tony up. I tried to give him one next and the same thing happened. Knowing that he was extremely upset we gave up and went over to the barn so we could watch him hopefully settle down. He didn't. Instead, Tipper continued in desperation to get out of his pen. His howling slowly turned into a sad moaning sound.

That evening, when Tony fed the dogs, we made Tipper up a special dinner of canned dog food, in hopes that he would forgive us. He didn't. Tipper howled throughout the night.

The next morning, as Tony cleaned the pens, I tried to make friends with Tipper once again. He growled at me as I approached and lunged at the gate when I got close. It was quite evident that he didn't want anything to do with me—ever! Before leaving his pen I noticed that he hadn't touched his dog food from this morning or from the night before, either, so I tossed a couple of hot dogs into his pen hoping that he would be hungry enough to eat them. He wasn't.

Around nine o'clock, Ben Welch showed up for work. We told him Tipper's story and asked him to try to make friends with him, since all of our dogs loved Ben. He grabbed some hot dogs and went to Tipper's pen. The same thing happened to Ben that had happened to us—Tipper went ballistic! Before leaving Tipper, Ben tossed the hot dogs into his pen and then walked away.

The three of us took turns, all day long, trying to get Tipper to like us. Nothing had changed, but we did notice that the hot dogs were missing, and that was a good sign.

Tipper howled most of that day and well into that night.

The following morning, Ben, Tony, and I had a meeting outside by the barn to try to figure out what to do about Tipper, because he was so unhappy. It came up in our conversation that maybe I should call the old man and tell him what was going on. We finally decided that we would give Tipper one more day before making that phone call.

It was decided that Tony would be the first to go by Tipper's pen and toss in a couple of hot dogs as he passed by it, then Ben would do it a few hours later, and then I would do it last. We decided that we would not try to talk to Tipper because it upset him so, and if we simply walked past his pen, not looking him in the eyes, and just tossed the hot dogs, he might look forward to our walk-bys.

Tony, Ben, and I have since jokingly argued who it was that came up with the brilliant idea of doing the walk-bys, but it really doesn't matter at all—it worked!

For two more days we continued our walk-bys without looking at or talking to Tipper; all we did was just sling hot dogs. By the end of the last day, Tipper was at the gate with his tail wagging, anxiously awaiting my walk-by. When I returned to the barn the three of us grabbed more hot dogs and went back to Tipper's alley to see if he would let us talk to him. He did!

We weren't sure if the three of us would be too much for him to handle, but we decided to go ahead and try. To our amazement, Tipper stood next to the gate, wagging his tail at us. We sat down next to the gate and started talking to him, as we took turns sticking hot dogs, one by one, through the gate into Tipper's mouth.

Tipper ate it up. He had finally come around!

Even though we know feeding hot dogs is not really the best of diets for dogs, we have learned over the years that they can be very useful in turning around a sad dog's disposition.

We spent around a half an hour talking to Tipper before going into his alley. He welcomed us with open paws when we opened the gate.

We were all ecstatic. Tipper took turns jumping up on each one of us to give a kiss, and, in return, we gave him more hot dogs. You'd think that he would be bloated by now, but he wasn't—he was just hooked on hot dogs as were the three of us.

We stayed with Tipper for about an hour, talking, laughing, petting, and feeding him more hot dogs. When we got ready to leave Tony asked Tipper to sit and Tipper sat. Then Tony asked him to give him a high-five, because the old man had told us that Tipper was well trained and knew how to do the high-five routine. Tipper, who was still sitting, looked at Tony, then at Ben and me, like he was thinking or trying to figure something out.

Then, out of nowhere, Tipper suddenly jumped up and slapped Tony's hand with his left paw! We all clapped and praised him for being so smart. Tipper wagged his tail with pride and seemed to be enjoying all of the attention he was receiving. Then Tony asked Tipper to sit again and then asked him for another high-five. Once again, Tipper jumped up, tail wagging wildly, and slapped Tony's hand with his other paw. We applauded him, petted him, and then fed him his last hot dog for the day.

That night Tipper didn't howl even though it was a full moon. And the next morning he was happy and so were we.

A week later, we had some adoptions and were able to move Tipper to a pen. Tony decided that his roommate would be ShyAnn, a sweet, black, furry medium-sized dog. In no time at all, the two of them hit it off and became the best of buddies.

On November 21, 2004, we had a surprise for Tipper—and it wasn't hot dogs.

The old man's daughter had called Kinky a few days earlier to ask him if we still had Tipper. Kinky told her yes and that he was doing fine, and then asked her why she had called.

The daughter told Kinky that her father's wife had just walked out on him, and she definitely wasn't going to be coming back! She said that the wife had been the one responsible for making her dad give up his dog because Tipper didn't like her. The daughter then went on to explain that she had made the call to Kinky in hopes that she could get Tipper reunited with her father, who was still broken-hearted over losing him.

Kinky told her yes and asked her to call me to work out the arrangements. She and I decided that on the morning of November 23, 2004, she would come to the rescue ranch, pick Tipper up, and drive him back to her dad in Junction, Texas, to surprise him!

On that day, two days before Thanksgiving, the woman arrived out at the rescue ranch on time. Before seeing Tipper, she and I had a talk. She told me everything that she had told Kinky and how excited she was about surprising her father with Tipper. I told her all about Tipper's heart being broken, and the two of us started to cry. Tony walked in on us crying and didn't know what to do—so he left to go give the dogs treats.

Next, Kinky showed up. He had come over to the rescue ranch for the adoption and to meet the old man's daughter. When he walked in on us crying he took off to go find Tony.

After the woman and I had boo-hooed the last tears, we went and found Kinky and Tony. While they visited I went inside the trailer to fill out the adoption papers for her to sign. When I wrote down the day's date, it hit me. Tipper had been with us for exactly one year; the old man had brought him to us one year ago to the day.

With the adoption papers in hand I went back outside. The woman read our contract and signed it. When I told her about Tipper being with us for exactly one year, she and I started crying again. Kinky and Tony left again.

When they returned Tipper was on the end of Tony's leash. The woman called his name and he flipped out with excitement. His tail was going ninety miles an hour as he dragged Tony to greet her, but then he stopped flat in his tracks about halfway there and turned around, dragging Tony back to his old pen. It seemed that he had forgotten something.

When Tipper reached his pen, he lowered his head and gave ShyAnn a kiss, as if telling her good-bye, and then he turned around and dragged Tony back to us.

Of course, the woman and I started crying again, and Kinky and Tony just stood there smiling at what they had just seen Tipper do—waiting for us to dry up. When the woman opened the door to her Cadillac, Tipper jumped in and was ready to go home. He knew what was happening to him.

Later that evening the woman phoned Kinky. She thanked him over and over again for what we had done and then told him that when her father came outside to the backyard and saw Tipper standing there with his tail wagging, he broke down in tears of happiness. He and Tipper had spent the day going on walks in the woods, and Tipper was presently sleeping in front of their fireplace while her father napped in his chair. She told Kinky it was the happiest that she had ever seen her father or Tipper—and then she started crying into the phone.

Sunrise, Sunset

On Monday morning, March 14, 2005, the best friend that I have ever had passed away peacefully in her sleep. She was a sweet little eighty-year-old lady who had lived her life to the fullest. She was a Gemini and extremely funny—she was a true clown.

I met her back in 1992, when I was living in Austin, Texas. After our first introduction to each other, she and I quickly became the best of friends.

I loved her so much! Besides being my confidante, she was my personal cheerleader and biggest fan. She made me feel that I could do no wrong, and her bubbly personality often lifted my spirits when I felt that life was not treating me so well. In other words, she was always there for me. For example, she was there when my husband passed away from cancer in 1995. She was by my side the day I bought my small ranch in Utopia, Texas. She was with me the day Kinky, Tony, and I decided to start the rescue ranch. She was at Tony's and my wedding. She helped me get through the loss of my mother. She was with me the day that we moved the rescue ranch from Utopia to Kinky's family ranch, Echo Hill. With her passing, a big chapter in my life has now been closed.

Besides being so very special to me for so many reasons, it is important to note that in her younger days she had been an incredible athlete, excelling in basketball, soccer, running, and swimming. She was also so charismatic that when she entered a room she would always become the center of attention immediately. To put it bluntly, everyone that she met loved her and wanted to be around her.

I have noticed that it is often the case that after someone has died, their loved ones left behind often tend to ignore or forget the many faults of and mistakes made by their deceased loved one. They tend to only remember the best of times and wind up making their dearly departed sound like some kind of a hero or saint—it's human nature.

To tell the truth, I have also been guilty of glorifying my dearly departed loved ones, too. Even though my friend was so great, she wasn't perfect. She had only two extremely annoying bad habits: farting and snoring.

In my fifty-four years on this planet, I have never known anyone that farted so much. I would venture to say that she passed gas at least once an hour—twenty-four times a day—every day! And she didn't seem to care at all about her nonstop farting, because it was something that had been passed down from generation to generation. Her loud snoring was also attributed to an inherited trait.

No, I must admit, she wasn't perfect—she was my guardian angel. And I hope the story about the Rainbow Bridge is true, because she is the first one that I want to see after I die, when I hopefully go up to heaven. Mom and Dad are tied for second place.

Her name was Yoda-Lady-Who Parker. Her nicknames were the Baby Yoda, Yo-Yo, or just Yo. My little farting machine was a black-and-white Boston Terrier. During our twelve wonderful years together, she inspired me to create cartoons and make cut-and-paste images of her, such as changing the face of the famous *Mona Lisa* to Yoda's and calling it the "Yoda Lisa," and changing *Whistler's Mother* to "Yo Mama," etc.

The morning that Yoda died, I was heartbroken, but I did not let myself cry until after I had finished doing the "Steve & Harley Show" on 94.3. I knew that I couldn't tell Steve and Harley about Yoda, because I would then fall apart and be unable to do the show because of my crying.

While I talked about the ranch to them on the air, Tony was outside in our front yard digging a grave for Yoda. The radio show went fine, but when I hung up the phone, I became a basket case and could not quit crying. I was already missing her farting and snoring.

When Tony came inside the trailer, he told me the grave was ready, and he too had tears in his eyes. I asked him to help me put Yoda inside one of my black Utopia Animal Rescue Ranch sweatshirts, and then we could bury her. He did exactly that, and then he carried her outside to her grave to be buried. I put her puppy collar, some flowers, and a note that I had written to her earlier that morning into the grave. Tony put in a brand new tennis ball.

Tony and I cried as he shoveled the dirt back into the grave. After that, we each told her good-bye and thanked her for all of the joy that she had brought into our lives. After I went inside, Tony placed heavy rocks on top of her grave to mark it.

That was one of the saddest days of my life, and I thank God that Tony was so understanding and helpful to me.

When Kinky called, Tony told him about Yoda's passing, and then handed me the phone and told me that Kinky wanted to talk to me. Kinky expressed his sympathies, said some very kind words about Yoda, and then reassured me that Yoda was already at the Rainbow Bridge waiting for me. His voice cracked as he said, "The only fault that dogs have is they don't live long enough." His kind words meant a lot to me, because I knew that he understood.

That night, I hardly slept a wink, because I missed Yoda's snoring and could not quit crying.

Horrors! The next morning when the sun came up, we discovered that wild hogs had come into the rescue ranch during the night and had tried to dig Yoda's body up! Her grave was a total wreck—fifty-pound rocks had been moved as far away as ten feet from her gravesite, but, fortunately, the hogs had not gotten to her body. It made me sick.

Tony immediately went outside and took care of everything. He put the grave back to the way that we had left it the day before. That day was much better for me, and I hardly shed a tear and was almost back on track as long as I didn't think of Yoda.

Double horrors! The next morning we discovered at dawn that the wild hogs had returned during the night and once again had tried to dig up Yoda's remains. Fortunately, the grave robbers' mission was not accomplished—they had failed miserably. Yoda's body was still in the ground.

I had had enough! When Tony returned to the trailer after cleaning the dog pens and feeding the dogs some treats, I announced that I was going to the Medina Ace Hardware Store to buy a couple of sacks of cement. I asked Tony if he would mind mixing up the cement and pouring a slab over the top of Yoda's grave, so the hogs couldn't dig up her body. Tony agreed to do it.

When I returned from Medina, Tony and Ben were waiting for me by Yoda's grave. They had built a three-foot square frame out of two-by-fours and had the wheelbarrow and watering hose ready to mix the cement. When I saw the square, I didn't like it, so I asked Tony and Ben if they could please make a three-foot-wide heart-shaped slab instead of the square one. I know that Ben and Tony thought I was crazy, but they agreed to make it a heart.

After about twenty minutes of setting up a heart form out of rocks, they went to work mixing the cement. While they did that, I was inside finding little things to set into the cement, like a silver dog bone and my cast steel, black-and-white flying pig that weighed at least twenty-five pounds. Tony and Ben carefully placed my bone and flying pig exactly where I wanted them into the quick-drying cement. When they had finished they stood up, and I thanked them for being so nice.

Then it hit me. I ran—well, skipped—into the trailer and went to our closet and opened the door. Thank goodness it was there! I found it on the top shelf; I grabbed the box. It was perfect for Yoda's grave.

"I found it! I found it!" I yelled with excitement as I half-stumbled down the porch to join up with Ben and Tony by Yoda's grave.

"What?" Tony asked.

"What?" Ben echoed.

"I bought this outdoor solar light," I said, "last week in Kerrville, and was going to use it as a last-minute birthday present if I needed one. Open it up!"

Ben ripped open the box, and he and Tony tried to hold back their laughter when they saw a ten-inch-tall amber glass squirrel holding an acorn staring back at them.

Thank goodness the cement had not fully set up. While Ben put the solar parts inside the squirrel, Tony sunk some screws down into the cement, so the squirrel could be bolted down. Finally, when Ben had the amber squirrel put together, he and Tony set it in place and screwed it down into the hardening cement.

It was perfect! I loved it! I thanked Tony and Ben and then went into the trailer to call Kinky to tell him what Tony and Ben had done for me and Yoda. By the sound of Kinky's voice, I could tell that he was think-ing I had lost my mind, but he didn't let on.

After our conversation, I went back outside to find that Tony and Ben had vanished; they were nowhere to be found. I guessed that they were hiding from me, thinking I might find something else for them to add to Yoda's shrine.

That evening, after the sun had hidden itself on the other side of the mountain, I went to the front door and looked outside. Right when I glanced at Yoda's grave the squirrel lit up with an amber glow. Seeing it made me simultaneously smile and tear up. From a distance it looked like a little flame.

"Tony," I said. "You have got to see this! The squirrel just lit up! I love it!"

Tony came out of his TV room and looked out the front door. "That's great, Nance," Tony said. "I'm glad that you like it."

"I'm going to call it the Eternal Squirrel! I've got to call Kinky and Ben and tell them!" I said.

I called Kinky over at the Lodge and told him about the Eternal Squirrel, and then he put me on the phone with Ben and I repeated myself about the Eternal Squirrel to him. They were both happy that I was happy, even though they had been about as enthusiastic as Tony had been. Before hanging up the phone, Kinky got back on the line and teased me about the three of them checking me into a psychiatric ward for observation. That conversation was ended with laughter.

To date, thanks to my good friends Steve and Harley, the Eternal Squirrel has become somewhat famous throughout the Texas Hill Country. Their loyal listeners have actually called me to ask if they could drive out with their families to see the Eternal Squirrel. They would tell me that they didn't want to adopt a dog, but they did want to see the Eternal Squirrel and have their pictures taken with it. In fact, Steve and Harley came out to the rescue ranch and we took pictures of them posing beside the Eternal Squirrel, and we posted it up on our website. They told me they would call their picture with the Eternal Squirrel, "The Eternal Squirrel with two nuts!"

My friends, too, have brought out people to the rescue ranch to see it and to prove to them that there really is an Eternal Squirrel that's in my front yard. And the most famous personality—besides Kinky, Steve and Harley, John Kelso, and Boomer the Dog—that has come out here just to see the Eternal Squirrel is Billy Joe Shaver.

I love the Eternal Squirrel, because every time that I see it, talk about it, or just think about it, it causes me to laugh. (Yoda would like that.)

The other night, when Tony and I were outside marveling at the Eternal Squirrel from our front porch, I jokingly remarked, "Tony, I've decided that from here on out, when a fart passes my way—it's Yoda saying hi."

Tony looked at me and began laughing. "I'm calling Kinky," he stated, before going inside our trailer.

Pryor-ity Male!

For over a month our ranch was back and forth on the phone to Jennifer Lee (Richard Pryor's wife) and her friends Karen and Shannon concerning a dog named Pierce, who had been abandoned in a front yard in Los Angeles with no food or water for days. He was approximately eight years old, and this was the second time he was abandoned. Jennifer and her friends rescued him and boarded him at a kennel for over three weeks while desperately trying to find Pierce a home.

No one would take Pierce because he had issues, such as being unpredictable and biting. (And, who could blame him? I'd bite too, if I had been treated like that.) The places they called suggested that he be euthanized because of his biting. Jennifer, Shannon, and Karen refused to heed the advice and kept on trying until Jennifer made a call to Kinky.

Kinky put them in touch with Tony and me and the rest is history. It took us about a week to line out a plan. First off, the ranch changed Pierce's name to Pryor in honor of Richard Pryor, whom we all love. Next, we worked out the transportation.

On Monday, April 5, 2004, Pryor departed LAX headed for his new home in Texas.

Below is an e-mail that I sent to Jennifer Lee, Richard Pryor, Karen, and Shannon the following day after Pryor's departure.

> Tuesday, April 6th . . . Good morning Jennifer, Richard, Karen and Shannon. Forgive me for not writing to each of you individually, but I only got about three hours of sleep last night and it was not Pryor's fault. First off, let me tell you how much Tony, Kinky and I love Pryor! Here is the way it went down last night and please remember that we were under a full moon, too! (Jennifer can explain the full moon deal to y'all later.)
>
> 6:30 p.m.: Tony and Maribeth Couch leave to go to the airport in San Antonio to pick up Pryor.
>
> 7:00 p.m.: Jennifer calls me and we visited for about ten minutes discussing Pryor.
>
> 8:00 p.m.: Kinky calls me and wants to be updated every 30 minutes or so on "Operation Airlift" or "Pryor-ity Mail!"
>
> 9:00–10:30 p.m.: I watch *Green Acres* reruns—hoping to distract myself from worrying about Pryor's arrival.
>
> 11:00 p.m.: Jennifer calls for an update on Pryor. Tony hadn't called, so I didn't have any news.
>
> 11:05 p.m.: I called Tony. He and Maribeth have just picked Pryor up and he never growled! Tony sounded relieved.
>
> 11:08 p.m.: I called Shannon and told her that "The Eagle Has Landed!"

11:15 p.m.: I called Jennifer and repeated myself about the eagle.

11:18 p.m.: I called Kinky to let him know that Pryor, Tony and Maribeth were headed our way.

11:20 p.m.: I began cooking Pryor's welcome home dinner. I cooked some hamburger with two eggs, green beans, cheese and garlic and mixed it all together. It smelled great!

11:21 p.m.: Kinky calls me while I am cooking—his back is killing him, but he wants to be here when Pryor arrives— so we make a plan.

[Please note: Ten days ago, Tony threw his back out. Eight days ago, I threw my back out, and three days ago, Kinky threw his back out, and not that this is real important, but one of our veterinarians, Dr. Wylie Skelton, threw his back out six days ago and so did our friend Jim Cravotta! I truly believe that throwing your back out can be contagious, but I don't think you can get it over the Internet.]

11:55 p.m.: Tony calls from Bandera (22 miles from us) and as we are talking on the phone the TV goes into an emergency weather forecast! Out of nowhere, some heavy thunderstorms showed up and they were headed straight for us! Dime-sized hail had hit Rocksprings which is only about 45 minutes/45 miles away. Wind shears up to 70 mph had also been clocked in Junction, Texas! Tony tells me that he is seeing lightning in our direction, but so far they hadn't run into any bad weather.

11:58 p.m.: My heart sinks over the forecast that I had just heard. I called Kinky to alert him and we now had become nervous wrecks concerning the weather reports. Kinky tells me that he is driving over here now.

12:10 a.m.: I meet Kinky outside in front of Pryor's pen. The winds had picked up and it was thundering and lightning and starting to rain. Kinky and I jumped into the Explorer and waited in silence for Tony and Pryor's arrival. Suddenly, he starts laughing and says, "Thank God Pryor isn't a giant dog! I can just see the three of us with our backs out—try-

ing to carry his cage." I laughed so hard that my back began
to hurt really bad.

12:15 a.m.: Tony and Pryor arrive! It was really starting to rain
cats and dogs as Tony, Kinky and I carried Pryor's cage from
the back of the truck to his new pen. If anybody had been
watching us, it looked like we were doing a poor imitation
of Harvey Korman, Tim Conway and Carol Burnett doing
a skit on old people. This is how it happened.

First off, Tony lowered the tail gate of the truck. Then the
three of us took our positions around Pryor's cage. On the
count of three, we shuffled our feet swiftly, in tiny baby
steps, to Pryor's pen and sat it down. Kinky and I then shuffled quickly out of the pen and Tony did the ribbon cutting. He reached down and unlatched Pryor's door. Before
Pryor came out of his cage, Tony had swiftly scooted outside of the pen. As the rain fell and the lightning cracked,
Pryor stretched, pooped, drank some water and then ate the
homemade dinner that I had cooked for him earlier.

12:30 a.m.: Satisfied that Pryor was going to be okay, Kinky
went home and we went back to our trailer. Ten minutes
later, all hell broke loose—thunder, lightning, high winds,
etc. Tony and I grabbed our raincoats, put on our rubber
boots, and went outside to the pens to check on the dogs.
Dustin Hoffman and Martha Stewart, two of our smaller
dogs, had escaped from their pens. After we had rounded
them up and had them safely back in their pens, Randy
Travis leaped out of his pen! After returning Randy to his
digs we went back to our trailer. We were so wound up
with the storm and all of the excitement, that neither one
of us could sleep, so we watched weather reports until we
did.

Tuesday, 9:00 a.m.: We wake up to find that Medina had
flooded over the night! We were all fine but the rivers and
creeks were over their banks. Fortunately, we are high up
and all we got from the flood—was mud! Unfortunately for
Kinky, he was stranded at his Lodge and out of cigars.

12:30 p.m.: All is well now. The rivers are going down and

Pryor, who I have fallen madly in love with, has already eaten two eggs with bacon for breakfast (laced with garlic). We have served him hot dog wieners every hour on the hour this morning and he seems to like the attention that he is receiving. He seems to be doing great and we are taking it very slowly with him. Here are some pics for y'all that I took this morning. Take care out there and be glad that I did this in *Reader's Digest* form.

Love to all, Nancy

P.S. Kinky is doing fine—he found three cigars!

Babe looking for Ruth

The Yoda Lisa

Getting ready for the mansion

PART THREE

Something to Crow About

Nick & Barbra Streisand Marsh

Buddies

Serenity

Kinky, Pretty Mama, &
Ben

Meanwhile, back at
the ranch

The Good, the Bad, and the Funny Bonefit

On Saturday, September 12, 1998, Kinky came out to visit our newly rescued dogs and to learn their names. While we were outside in the pens, musician Butch Hancock and his family showed up at the rescue ranch to take the very first official tour.

During the tour, Butch suggested that we call our upcoming benefits "bonefits." We loved the idea, and that is how we came up with that name.

In early January 1999, I went over to Kinky's to pick up Mr. Magoo to babysit him, because Kinky was flying off to Samoa to get some writing done. Before I left with Magoo, Kinky told me that he would be unreachable by phone for about ten days, once he left Hawaii for Samoa, and he had put Cleve Hattersley in charge of our first Bonefit. I was glad that Cleve was going to handle the Bonefit for us, but I wasn't particularly happy about Kinky being unreachable for ten days, because we usually talked daily to each other; it really bothered me, but little did I know what a problem that was going to be.

Just a few days after Kinky was officially in Samoa came trouble with a capital "T!" My brother, Ron, called to tell me that our friends Sammy Allred and Bob Cole, who host the number-one morning radio talk show in Austin on KVET, were badmouthing Cleve, Kinky, the rescue ranch, and our upcoming Bonefit. After their show was over calls came pouring in from their listeners wanting to know what was going on. I didn't have a clue, so I called Cleve, since I couldn't reach out and touch someone who was on the other side of the planet.

When I finally reached Cleve he was beside himself. He couldn't decide if he should hang himself or shoot himself in the noggin. He told me that Sam and Bob were upset because "we" had asked some other radio station to promote and sponsor our event instead of them. Cleve then went on to explain that he had assumed that Kinky had already talked to Sam and Bob about our Bonefit, and that was why he had contacted the other radio station. It was simply a little matter of miscommunication.

While Kinky was busy tickling the keys of his typewriter in Samoa, Sam and Bob were busy taking snipes at Kinky, Cleve, and the rescue ranch—every morning! With each day that passed, "the war of words" escalated to the point that Kinky's friend Don Imus picked up on it and jumped right into the middle of it on his "Imus in the Morning" show.

Every day, when Sam and Bob would blast us, Imus would fire right back. It seemed that this little matter of miscommunication had now escalated to mass communication. It seemed that the whole world knew about the feud—except for Kinky.

Rumor had it that one morning Imus asked his listening audience to call Sam and Bob and give them an earful. It was reported back to us that there were so many phone calls that it actually blew up their switchboard!

Nine days later, when our Gandhi-like figure finally phoned home from the only phone on the island, the connection was bad and so was our conversation. After being briefed as to what had been going on, Kinky immediately flew back to Texas to try to fix things.

This was the first time that I realized that Kinky was not a handyman at fixing everything that needed mending. It seemed that the harder that Kinky tried to repair relations between Sam and Bob and Imus, the worse matters got. At one point, one of Kinky's best friends, John McCall, flew Sammy up to New York City in his private jet so Sammy could be on the "Imus in the Morning" show to work things out with Imus and Kinky.

That show was really great. Imus had Sammy in the studio and the Kinkster on the phone. The three of them spent the morning trying to straighten things out, but the only thing that the three of them did jokingly agree on that morning was that Cleve was a genius.

Kinky at one point exclaimed, "There's something about a benefit that brings out the worst in everybody."

Sammy chimed in, "No good deed goes unpunished."

After all was said and done, thanks to the I-Man and John McCall, a cease-fire was declared before the morning radio show ended!

A couple of hours after that show had aired, the rescue ranch received a very important call. When I answered the phone, Greg Underwood introduced himself and told me that he had just seen the Imus show on MSNBC and was also a big fan of Kinky's. He then went on to say that he had no idea our rescue ranch even existed until he heard about us earlier that morning on Imus. He asked me a lot of questions about the rescue ranch and Kinky, and then, near the end of our conversation, told me that he wanted to help the rescue ranch. He asked me if we needed dog food, and, of course, my answer was yes. Greg then asked me if we ever used Hill's Science Diet, and I told him no—because we simply couldn't afford it. To my surprise, Greg explained that he worked for Hill's Science Diet and would be sending down a truckload of dog food within the next few days! I was so excited about this news I told Greg that I was going to call Kinky and ask him to give him a call. Now Greg got excited, because he could not believe that Kinky would actually be calling him.

Well, Kinky called Greg to thank him immediately after I had phoned him, and the rest is history—Greg Underwood is now a good friend of ours and a hero to our dogs.

What I call a truckload, and what Greg Underwood calls a truckload, are two entirely different things. When the Hill's Science Diet truck arrived in downtown Utopia, Tony's and my jaws dropped—it was an eighteen-wheeler! We had to quickly rent two storage units from Utopia Mini-Storage, and we also had to borrow forklifts from Utopia Builders Supply and Utopia Sales and Service Company to unload the free twenty-three thousand pounds of dog food. Our friends Ernie Moore and T-Bone Couch volunteered their services by operating the forklifts. In less than an hour, the eighteen-wheeler was empty and our storage units were packed full. Knowing that the rescue ranch dogs would now be eating one of the best dog foods that money can buy made that day one that we'll never forget.

On March 5, 1999, five days before the Bonefit, the rescue ranch received a very generous donation from Don Imus and his family, along with some beautifully embroidered jackets that Don and his brother Fred Imus had sent to be auctioned off at our silent auction. Because I was trying to keep up with everything that was going on, I stupidly sent Don Imus a thank-you form letter. As soon as I had mailed the darn letter, I immediately knew that I should have included a personal note expressing our gratitude instead of using our standard form letter. In fact, I even confessed to Kinky about my mistake, and he agreed with me that I should have written a note, but it was too late—the damage was fixin' to be done.

Wednesday morning, March 10, 1999, the day of our Bonefit, Tony and I were watching the Imus show, when Don held up my form letter and started blasting me! He used every bad name that he could think of to describe me for being so impersonal and unprofessional. I felt absolutely horrible, even though I knew that I deserved his wrath. After dragging me through the mud all across the country, I decided to fax Don a full apology immediately. I wrote him an apology and agreed with him about me being a moron and unprofessional. I finished off the letter by telling Don that today was supposed to have been so great, because Tony and I were secretly getting married at our ranch and we hadn't even told Kinky yet. Then, like a fool, I faxed my letter off to Don. Mistake number two—and, as they say, "and she's stupid, too!"

When Don received my fax, he read it out loud and everyone in the studio was laughing at me. Then Kinky phones me from Austin and tells me to never, ever send Don another letter or fax, and then he congratulates me on Tony's and my soon-to-be marriage! Looking back now it was all so very funny and I deserved exactly what I got from Don.

At ten o'clock sharp, our friend Bill Schaefer, the justice of the peace in Utopia, arrived to marry Tony and me. We said our vows to one another outside by the dog pens. After officially getting hitched we left for Austin.

We were three hours early for the event when we arrived in Austin at La Zona Rosa. When Kinky saw us, he came over and hugged us both, and then quickly introduced us to Cleve, who was busily supervising the volunteers and making sure everything was set and ready to go.

Next, Kinky took us to meet the MSNBC crew that Imus had sent down to document our Bonefit. Later on that evening, with Steve Rambam and Kinky standing next to me, the camera crew turned on their cameras and this is what Kinky had to say: "This is Cousin Nancy. Nancy got married this morning. Imus made Nancy cry because she sent him a form letter . . ." Then he finished off with, "When I talked to Don earlier today and told him that he had made Cousin Nancy cry on her wedding day, Don said, "_____ Cousin Nancy!"

With that said we all broke out laughing; it was hilarious!

That night the energy at La Zona Rosa was electrifying. Everybody seemed to be up and enjoying themselves. The silent auction was a big hit, too. We auctioned off John McCall's Jackie Onassis saddle, an autographed pair of Dwight Yoakam's cowboy boots, and Willie Nelson's golf cart, among many other great items.

The music could not have been any better either. Jerry Jeff Walker was the headliner for our event, and when he sang "Mr. Bojangles" and "Redneck Mother" I thought the crowd was going to go through the ceiling. Every singer and musician was incredibly great, and below is the list of all of the performers that helped out our rescue ranch for free: Jerry Jeff Walker and the Lost Gonzo Band, Robert Earl Keen, Joe Ely, Marcia Ball, Jimmie Dale Gilmore, Ray Benson, Lee Roy Parnell, James McMurtry, the Austin Lounge Lizards, Butch Hancock, the Geezinslaw Brothers, Kacey Jones, Double Trouble, Stephen Bruton, Alvin Crow, Ponty Bone, Sweet Mary and her young violinists, Trish Murphy, Sarah Elizabeth Campbell, Ana Egge, Lisa Hattersley, and Kinky Friedman and Little Jewford.

Our celebrity hosts for the evening were Mayor Kirk Watson, Molly Ivins, Cactus Pryor, Rep. Elliott Naishtat, Bud Shrake, Turk Pipkin, Johnny Marks, Kevin Connor, Steve Alex and Harley Belew, and Little Jewford.

And, to top it all off, our Honorary Event Chairwoman was, at the time, the First Lady of Texas—Laura W. Bush and her dog Spot.

Our first Bonefit was magical, and the people we met that night have become good friends and supporters of our rescue ranch. Jeremy Newberger reported back to Imus the following morning that Kinky, Sammy, and Cleve had buried the hatchet, and the event was a financial success. The following Memorial Day Weekend, Imus had MSNBC air our Bonefit to the world, which caused a landslide of phone calls, donations, and adoptions.

After serving out Kinky's imposed one-year probation banning me from having any contact with Don, Kinky finally decided to lift it after I had learned my lesson well. I now always include a short note with anything that I send to the I-Man or anyone else who has significantly helped our rescue ranch—it's called etiquette.

The Dwight Night

Friday, December 17, 1999, Kinky called to tell me that he had just gotten off of the phone with Dwight Yoakam, and Dwight had agreed to do a Bonefit for the rescue ranch. The only open date that Dwight had was Saturday, March 25, 2000. With that great news, the wheels were set in motion.

On January 3, 2000, Kinky, Tony, and I drove to Helotes, Texas, to meet up with Cleve Hattersley, from Austin, and the owner of the John T. Floore Country Store, Steve McLaughlin, to discuss and plan our Bonefit. After a brief meeting, Steve pulled out his *Farmer's Almanac* to find out if the weather was going to cooperate with our scheduled outdoor event.

Steve explained to us that he always consults his almanac before booking any event, to make sure that the weather would be conducive for an outdoor concert. He then went on to tell us that the almanac had never let him down—it had always been right on the money concerning the weather for their concerts.

We all held our breaths until Steve confirmed that that Saturday night would be perfect—no rain was forecast and the outside temperature would be ideal. With that news, we all shook hands. Because the rescue ranch was low in funds, Kinky, our Gandhi-like figure, wrote checks from his personal bank account: one for Cleve to get things rolling, and the other check for Steve to nail down and cement the date, March 25, 2000, for our Bonefit.

Following the meeting at Floore's, Kinky, Cleve, Tony, and I ate lunch at the Chaparral in Helotes. Over chips and salsa, it was decided that Kinky would ask Don Imus to be our Honorary Chairperson. Over tacos, Cleve agreed that he would get the publicity out and handle the event. By the time we had run out of flour tortillas, we all knew what each of us had to take care of.

Things began snowballing at the rescue ranch, as the days rolled on towards our event. The rescue ranch was receiving, on the average, forty phone calls a day from people wanting more information about the concert or to volunteer for that night, or from the media wanting to come out to do a story on us. Kinky was being bombarded with interviews, and the rescue ranch hosted one camera crew after another wanting to do stories to help us. Even though it was somewhat exhausting, it was very exciting.

On the day of the Bonefit, Don Imus sent down his crew to cover our event. Around noon, Kinky, Little Jewford, Jeff and Mary Erramouspe, Bethany Clark, Ted Mann, Brian Alstott and his sister, Marlene, Patrick and Janice O'Sullivan, Dori Bailin and her sister, Don and Carol Linse, Brian Donovan and the MSNBC crew, and many others arrived out at the rescue ranch. Jeff and Mary made sandwiches for our guests, and Bethany was put in charge of trailer security, while Kinky, Tony, Little Jewford, and I gave a grand tour of the rescue ranch with the MSNBC cameras rolling. And, of course, Kinky and Little Jewford were absolutely hilarious!

By 2:30 p.m., all of our guests left the ranch headed for Helotes. When Tony and I arrived at Floore Country Store, around 5:30 p.m., a line of ticket holders, approximately a mile long, were waiting patiently for the doors to open at 6:00. The sky was filled with dark, fast-moving clouds, and the weather forecaster had predicted showers for the evening.

Even though I am a Libra, it was hard for me to hide my worries concerning the weather forecast. When Kinky came up, he saw right through me and said, "Don't worry, Nance. It is out of our control now. The Lord will provide." Little did I know he was right.

While Cleve nervously directed our volunteer friends Patrick O'Sullivan and Roger Robinson on taking care of the final touches, Dwight arrived, and so did the entire Helotes Police Department that we had hired for the event. The place was getting busier and busier by the minute.

By six o'clock, the doors opened up, and the clouds vanished into thin air!

Promptly at seven o'clock, Two Tons of Steel took the stage to kick off the night's event. Of course, they were great. Then came the Derailers, who had everyone dancing. Next, Joe Ely came on stage and had the crowd roaring when he sang, "Hound Dog!" Following his great performance, Ruth Buzzi, Lou Ferrigno, who played the Incredible

Hulk on TV from 1978–1982, Little Jewford, and Kinky had the folks screaming with laughter as they cut up on stage. After they had finished, the Geezinslaw Brothers' performance was fabulous, and the crowd went wild! The audience was electrified.

After their performance, Sammy Allred introduced Dwight Yoakam. When Dwight came out on stage, the crowd howled so loudly with excitement that I would bet that the citizens of San Antone, some twenty miles away, could hear them. Dwight was absolutely incredible—he outdid himself that night, and the audience knew it. When Flaco Jiménez joined Dwight up on stage, to top off the show, the electricity flowing through the crowd was so strong that it gave me goose bumps.

Following the concert we all agreed that Dwight's Bonefit was a smashing success.

What I Like about Texas

One of Texas's favorite singer-songwriters, Gary P. Nunn, became an official Ranch Hand at our ranch on Sunday, July 2, 2000.

Months before, Gary's roadie, and our good friend, Roger Robinson, had talked to Gary about our rescue ranch, and Gary had told him that he wanted to do something to help our animals. That was all that Roger needed to hear. He called us to tell us the good news, promising that he would take care of everything, and we set the date right then.

Early Sunday morning, Roger arrived at our rescue ranch with his wife, Patti, and their children, Ian and Jessica, to get things ready for Gary's meet-and-greet. Within a couple of hours everything was done. All we needed was Gary.

Kinky arrived a couple of hours later, along with our many friends from Utopia, including some of Gary's fans from Houston. Gary was running late, so Kinky gave everyone a tour of the rescue ranch and then visited with our crowd. We were glad that Gary was not on time because one of his fans who had driven up from Houston adopted one of our sweet dogs—Tacy!

Unable to reach Gary by cell phone, Roger became concerned about him, because Gary was never late for a gig. Fortunately, Roger's worries were soon put to rest when two trucks came flying down the dusty dirt road headed for the rescue ranch. The lead truck was Lindy Padgett's, and the second pickup was Gary's.

When they arrived, Lindy, who drives like a wild woman, explained to us that Gary had gotten lost and had come into Heaven's Landing, where she works, to ask for directions to the rescue ranch. Knowing it was faster to bring Gary here than to give him directions, she locked up the shop and brought him to us.

Even though Gary was a little shocked by how fast Lindy had driven, he chatted with Kinky for a minute before grabbing his guitar case and coming over to meet everyone. After everyone shook his hand, Gary sat down with his guitar and asked if there were any requests. I immediately asked him to play my all-time Gary P. Nunn favorite, "What I Like about Texas"! When he finished the song, he got a standing ovation, and our dogs went into a howl. With every request that Gary played, our dogs would howl when the applause came. Among the many songs that he sang, my favorites were "Uncle Bud," "The Domino Song," and "Gracias Por Ese"—not to mention, his famous "London Homesick Blues."

An hour later, after Gary had sung his final song for us, Kinky told Gary, in front of everybody, that as a thank-you to him, Gary could adopt any one of our super dogs. Graciously, Gary declined Kinky's offer by telling us that he and his wife, Ruthie, had guineas, horses, ducks, chickens, cows, donkeys, goats, sheep, cats, and several dogs on their ranch in Oklahoma. "Our motto at our ranch is: We feed 'em, and don't eat 'em," Gary joked, as he packed up his guitar before leaving.

Niles and Niles of Texas

On August 3, 1999, Robert Earl Keen came to our rescue ranch to bring us his mother's dog Roscoe, because his mother had to be placed in a nursing home and could no longer care for her dog. Robert Earl and his wife, Kathleen, loved Roscoe, but they already had too many dogs, so they could not keep him. Kathleen phoned Kinky to ask for help, and Kinky, of course, said yes.

When Tony and I first met Robert Earl outside our trailer, I couldn't tell who was sadder—Robert Earl or Roscoe. Because everyone knows what Robert Earl Keen looks like, I shall describe Roscoe. He was a huge, ninety-pound, sweet, ten-year-old dog who was sad but still full of love—definitely an old soul. When Robert Earl introduced us to Roscoe, this magnificent dog, who had lost the love of his life, managed to wag his tail at us.

Tony and Robert Earl took Roscoe to a pen that Tony had earlier made ready for him, and then left Robert Earl and Roscoe alone so they could say their good-byes to each other. A while later, Robert came back to our trailer with his eyes wet and handed us a check for helping Roscoe. Then filled with sadness, Robert Earl drove away.

Roscoe was such a good sport about his situation that he immediately made friends with his roommates and got along fine with them. If their playing was too much for him he would walk away and go to his doghouse to rest. Everyone who met this great old dog fell in love with him.

In a short matter of time, Roscoe seemed happy and content with his new home and his playmates. Even though Kinky, Tony, and I try not to show favoritism, Roscoe stole our hearts—especially Tony's.

Every day, Tony would give Roscoe an extra dog treat and spend time sitting with him and talking to him. They were buddies. And I always knew when Tony was in Roscoe's pen, because Roscoe's bark sounded like a foghorn.

Even though Roscoe stole the potential adopters' hearts, no one wanted him because he was too old and on medications. But that did not seem to bother Roscoe—he remained happy for over a year-and-a-half, until he had a serious stroke.

Just before dark, Tony had gone out to check on the dogs and found Roscoe on the ground trying to get to his feet. Tony carried him to his doghouse and put him inside it so he could rest. When Tony came inside the trailer, tears were running down his face, and he was very depressed. He told me that Roscoe had had a stroke and seemed partially paralyzed, but his spirit was good, and he did not seem to be in any pain.

The next morning, the first thing that Tony did was to go check on his pal, Roscoe. To Tony's delight, he found Roscoe standing up on all fours, barking happily, and wagging his tail excitedly at Tony when he entered his pen. Roscoe was going to be fine! Tony told me later that it was like Roscoe was trying to tell him, "Look! I'm okay!" That was a very good morning.

That afternoon, I telephoned Kathleen to tell her about Roscoe's stroke and reassured her that he was fine and doing well. The rescue ranch received another generous donation the following day from Kathleen and Robert Earl.

A few weeks later, Kinky called us to tell us some exciting news. Kathleen Keen had just called him to tell him that she and Robert Earl wanted to help out the rescue ranch. Kinky went on to explain that Robert Earl would give a private, outdoor acoustic concert for one hundred and fifty of their friends, and their guests at Niles Wine Bar in San Antonio, giving all of the proceeds to our rescue ranch. And, the best part was Kathleen would handle the entire event, and all that we needed to do was to show up on April 26, 2001.

The day of the concert, after feeding the dogs and cleaning the pens, Tony and I were ready to drive to San Antonio for the private concert. Earlier, Kinky had talked us into staying overnight in San Antonio, so Maribeth came to our rescue and arrived with her suitcase in hand; we left her in charge of the rescue ranch. As we pulled out, Maribeth told us not to worry about the dogs and for us to have a good time.

We arrived a couple of hours before the concert at Niles Wine Bar— just minutes ahead of Kinky. Niles Chumney, the owner of the bar, immediately introduced himself to us, and he and his staff made us all feel very welcome. One beer later, Kathleen arrived to get everything ready for the concert. Before our second beer, Kathleen had placed Tony and me at a table near the door with our pamphlets, so we could answer any questions about the rescue ranch. Kinky was supposed to have stayed with us, but when the doors were opened to their guests, he was immediately swarmed by them wanting autographs, etc.

Then, when Robert Earl Keen arrived, it was showtime. With over two hundred people seated outdoors under a starlit sky, Kathleen took to the stage and asked everyone to please donate generously to our rescue ranch. Then she introduced Kinky as the Master of Ceremonies.

Kinky then took the stage and thanked Kathleen and Robert Earl, Niles and his staff, and the audience, and then read to the crowd his hilarious *Texas Monthly* story about living with a cat and four dogs. As Kinky read, we could hardly hear him because the audience was laughing so loudly. By the time he had finished his reading, Tony and I were surrounded by people making donations to the rescue ranch—and the night was still young!

Kinky then introduced Robert Earl Keen, and Robert Earl had the crowd in his hands before he even finished his first song. As loudly as the crowd had laughed at Kinky's story, you could have heard a pin drop as Robert Earl sang one song after another.

It was a magical night; there could not have been a better crowd, the weather was perfect, and, when the concert ended, the audience begged for an encore. In fact, looking back, there were actually two encores, and Robert Earl gave them exactly what they wanted. He sang "The Road Goes on Forever" and "Copenhagen."

What a night, and what great friends!

A little over a month later, on the morning of May 28th, Tony went out to the pens to feed the dogs and to clean the pens. He immediately knew something was wrong when he did not hear Roscoe's routine welcoming bark. He rushed to Roscoe's pen and found him curled up inside his doghouse sleeping. When Tony bent down to wake him, he discovered that his best friend had passed away during the night. With tears in his eyes, Tony buried Roscoe, along with his white Utopia Animal Rescue Ranch ball cap, under a large live oak tree, just outside Roscoe's pen. That was not a good day for us.

Afternoon Delight

Our luncheon in Austin, Texas, on May 29, 2002, at the Four Seasons Hotel with First Lady Laura Bush was a howling success! Texas's favorite Top Dogs and dignitaries from as far away as Vietnam attended our Bonefit.

Before the show started, Laura graciously let everyone attending our luncheon have the opportunity to have their picture taken with her. I felt sorry for the First Lady, because Laura had to take snapshot after snapshot with hundreds of people. I guess that goes with the territory and is part of what she does. And she did a great job, too.

At high noon, Kinky unleashed our fun event by barking to the crowd, "Folks, it's been a financial pleasure. We raised $125,000, but unfortunately we have spent $124,000 on the yogurt drizzle dessert!"

The entertainment would have won any "Best in Show," too. Little Jewford (Jeff Shelby) serenaded the crowd on the piano as our vegetarian dinners were served. Steve Fromholz cracked up the crowd with his vegetarian remark, "If God had meant for us to be vegetarians he wouldn't have made animals out of meat." He was followed by a beautiful solo by Austin's legendary violinist Sweet Mary Hattersley. Turk Pipkin did a reading of *Old Yeller* while escaping from a straitjacket. Sandra Brown entertained the crowd with an extremely funny story about a dog and a Dixie cup. Laura's favorites, Delbert McClinton and Tish Hinojosa, sang to everyone's delight. Liz Carpenter and Tom Friedman told some funny stories, and everyone thoroughly enjoyed Steve Harrigan's story about his love-hate relationship with a rabbit. A tear came to many eyes as Sammy Allred, on mandolin, accompanied Kinky singing "Marilyn and Joe." (It wasn't just their performance—it was because it was a beautiful love song.) Steve Rambam was so touched by Kinky's and Sammy's performance, he came over to my table during their performance and generously made a donation for a house to be built for our six non-partisan pigs! The only thing Steve requested was that it be named "Rambam's International House of Pigs."

But Laura brought the house down when she presented her hilarious slide show about her and George's White House dogs, Barney and Spot. She had the crowd roaring with laughter, including the Secret Service. Everyone agreed that it was the funniest slide show they had ever seen, and the best luncheon that they had ever attended.

Note to Laura

June 10, 2002

Dear Laura,

This morning while I was outside with the animals with Kinky, a little voice inside or maybe it was because Kinky was there, told me to come inside my trailer and pen you a note. So, here I am while Kinky remains outside huffing and puffing.

A cloud of smoke is slowly rising above our newly built pig house—"Rambam's International House of Pigs." It isn't a fire. It is just Kinky visiting our non-partisan pigs. His next stop will be my trailer.

Time is short. So, on behalf of Tony, the animals, our imaginary elephant, Mamajello, and myself, I want to thank you for doing our luncheon! It was an incredibly fun, exciting and successful event!

Everyone is saying and I must agree, that it was "the greatest thing to ever have happened for our animals and our rescue ranch!" Thank you, so very much! I must go— he is knocking on my door.

Sincerely with love—
Nancy Parker-Simons
Executive Director

Cowboy Up

For many years, Kinky and the rescue ranch have participated in the annual "Biggest Little Parade in Texas" in Center Point, Texas. Our good friends Jim and Liz Cravotta were the ones responsible for getting Kinky and the rescue ranch involved in celebrating this fun tradition.

The Saturday following the Fourth of July, every year, Texans come from all over the state to participate in or to watch this fun event. On many occasions, Kinky has been the Grand Marshall, which requires riding in the back of a decorated pickup holding a foghorn in one hand and throwing candy at children with the other. Even though his aim is excellent, he has missed a few but has never put any kid's eye out—yet.

One year, I rode in the back of the pickup with Kinky, and it was a lot of fun. While he chunked candy, I tossed doggie treats to the many dogs that lined the street. Tony was in that same parade, too, riding Harry and Vickie Gartrell's mule, Little Bit.

Following every parade, we always go to Harry and Vickie's house, along with a bunch of their friends, to celebrate with a Bloody Mary. This is always one of my favorite things to do, because Vickie and Harry have a wide assortment of animals that live in their house. The most unusual one is their llama, Dolly Llama, who roams from room to room in their home and occasionally sits down on their couch. Then there is their big, beautiful Cockatoo, Waldo, who walks around chattering and mumbling to himself, if he's not accompanying their baby grand player piano. Every time after leaving their home, I feel like I've just come out of Dr. Dolittle's world.

A couple of years ago, Kinky was unable to participate in the parade, so Tony and I went instead. When we arrived at Harry and Vickie's ranch, Liz and Jim quickly decorated the rescue ranch pickup with Kinky banners and signs that they had made. It looked fantastic.

It was decided that Jim would drive our truck, and I would ride shotgun and toss candy to the youngsters. When Tony was asked to ride in the back of the truck with a very pretty young woman, he gladly accepted his plight and even promised not to let her out of his sight. He kept his word.

When it was time to line up for the parade, a group of about fifteen men, the *charros*, took their position behind our truck on their horses. Jim and I got to laughing hysterically as we watched Tony staring at this glamorous young lady, while the charros all grinned and stared at her in the back of the pickup. At one point, one of the Mexican cowboys rode up so close that his horse's head was literally inside the back of the pickup.

When the parade started, Jim and I could not quit laughing at Tony or the charros. Every time that this young woman would bend down to get more candy to throw, the eyes of the cowboys would grow bigger, along with their smiles. Then, to our surprise, bystanders began yelling at Tony things like, "We love you, Kinky!"

Tony was literally in hog heaven! He would wave back to them with his cowboy hat and did a good job pretending to be Kinky. By the time the parade was over, tears were falling from both Jim's and my eyes—from laughter.

When we stopped to let Tony and this real-life Barbie doll get out of the bed of the pickup, the charros were still right behind us. In fact, one of them accidentally rear-ended us with his horse. That is not against the law in Texas, so we didn't bother calling the sheriff.

On the way back to the Gartrell's ranch, we teased Tony nonstop. And, because Tony is a Leo, he didn't seem to appreciate our humor or our jokes. It was a sad moment for Tony when we had to say our good-byes. I am positive that if he and I had not been married, he would of proposed to her in the back of the truck while the cowboys stared and drooled at her.

When we returned to the rescue ranch, we went to see Kinky to tell him about the parade. Kinky got a kick out of hearing my rendition of the events that took place, and Tony didn't seem to mind—his thoughts were elsewhere.

Over the River and up to Hill's

The place to be on Tuesday, September 23, 2003, was at Bob Cole's Hill's Cafe in Austin, Texas. Bob, Sammy Allred's most popular morning talk show partner on KVET, approached Kinky about wanting to do a benefit for the rescue ranch at his famous café in South Austin, Hill's.

With the help of Bob Cole and his crew, Kinky, Ben Welch, and his friends, we had another great Bonefit! Like magic, the weather was perfect for our outdoor fund-raiser when the doors opened up to the public at 5:00 p.m. Bob Cole and Kinky traded the microphone back and forth introducing the bands that night. They also teased the crowd that there was going to be a mystery guest showing up that night to perform.

The first band to play was Rivertrain, and they were fantastic. The Kings of the Motel 6 were next, and they were so good the crowd didn't want them to stop playing their music. When Austin favorite Honeybrowne took to the stage, they proved with their slick licks and tighter-than-tight band what great music is supposed to sound like.

Even though Honeybrowne was a hard act to follow, Kinky and Little Jewford took the stage, telling their jokes and getting the whole crowd to sing "Ole Ben Lucas" with them as Sweet Mary accompanied them. By the end of their act, everyone was laughing so hard they had tears in their eyes. My older sister, Cindy Roche, who was sitting at our table, actually laughed so hard she threw her back out.

I was in the restroom checking out my sister's back when the legendary gypsy songman Jerry Jeff Walker stepped up on the stage; the applause from the crowd outside made the bathroom walls shake, causing a couple of rolls of toilet paper to fall off the shelf and hit Cindy in the head. Back outside, with Cindy's back out, we watched Jerry Jeff give the crowd one super, incredible performance. As he sang one song after another, the audience became mesmerized by him and his talent.

Well, like father, like son; Django Walker took the stage, and, following in his dad's footsteps, showed the crowd what he was made of. In his own unique style, Django had everyone smiling and wanting to hear more of his music. He is a legend fixin' to happen.

Before Cory Morrow took the stage, Sweet Mary accompanied Sammy Allred and Kinky on her violin, performing one of my favorite Kinky songs, "Marilyn and Joe," a beautiful love song. They did such a great job that my sister, Cindy, had tears in her eyes. Then Cory Morrow jumped up on the stage and let us have it. To put it in one word, he was supercalifragilisticexpialidocious! But seriously, Mary Poppins would have floated away with delight with his performance.

To end the star-studded evening of spectacular entertainment, Kevin Fowler had the crowd howling with excitement before he even played one lick on his guitar or sang one note. I'm positive that the house would have come down if there had been a house anywhere near us under that big Texas sky. Everybody was dancing and singing his songs with him, and it could not have gotten any better that night—never!

Well, as that old saying goes, "never say never"—you're not going to believe what happened next. My good friends Larry Peters and his wife, Dee, rushed over to me to tell me that they had just spotted Dwight Yoakam going backstage with his guitar! Their news was unbelievable to me; the three of us took off to go backstage to check it out. Before we reached the backstage area, Dwight jumped out onto the stage and began playing along with Kevin. Everybody went nuts—Dwight Yoakam was the mystery guest! The unsuspecting crowd was screaming, hollering, and whistling in delight. And I am sure that I was not the only one who had gotten goose bumps.

Backstage, our good friend Harley Belew, from KRVL in Kerrville, found me and asked if I had brought my camera with me, because he wanted to have his picture taken with Dwight. My answer, of course, was yes. As Kevin and Dwight gave the crowd more than their money's worth, Tony made his way backstage and found us. Then the five of us made our way to the balcony beside the stage and watched the two great performers polish off the night.

When the show ended, Dwight and Kevin signed autographs and had their pictures taken with their fans. By the time Dwight returned to the backstage area, it was time for me to pull out my camera. I took pictures of Dwight with my friends Larry and Dee Peters; next, Jon and Sandy Wolfmueller; then, Harley Belew; and, last, Kinky. Then I handed my camera over to Tony and asked him to please shoot me. Kinky overheard me and told Tony not to shoot me until he had rounded up Jerry Jeff and Dwight. It was a Sony moment for me! Tony took a picture of Jerry Jeff Walker, Dwight Yoakam, Kinky, and me all standing together.

That night was sorta like a family reunion for me. I got to see my family, old friends, and visit and meet many of our supporters. Our Bonefit was a huge success because of the musicians, who volunteered their time and played their hearts out for our dogs that night, and also because of our good friends Bob Cole, Hill's Cafe, Sammy Allred, Ben Welch, Cleve Hattersley, Shirley Wetzel, Jerry and Sue Agiewich of Kinky Friedman's Private Stock Salsas, KVET, Harley Belew from KRVL, Gus and Linda Voelzel, and Jeff and Mary Erramouspe.

The following afternoon, my sister, Cindy, called to tell me that she and her husband, Ray, had a blast at the Bonefit, and that her back was feeling much better.

Steve & Harley

The "Six Million Dollar Dog"

Dottie West

PART FOUR

Friends—That's What It's All About

By Day

Mr. Magoo

Little Ricky Ricardo

Kinky feeding Roy & Gabby

Nelda & Jeepers

Angels from Helotes

L ittle did we know that the first time that Tony and I met Paul Emerson, he not only would become our first volunteer, but also one of our best friends.

In the spring of 1999, shortly after our first Bonefit was held up in Austin, Paul drove out to the rescue ranch. He had heard about us from an article that he had recently read in the newspaper, and, because he was an avid animal lover, he wanted to check us out.

When Paul showed up at the rescue ranch, he was packing—and no, he wasn't wearing a gun—he was loaded with several boxes of doggie treats to give out to our dogs. The tour we gave Paul lasted a lot longer than usual, because he wanted to get into every dog pen and personally meet, and pet, every single dog that we had. Our dogs loved it!

That day, before Paul departed the rescue ranch, he asked us if it would be okay for him to come out the next weekend and visit the dogs again. Our answer, of course, was yes—and he did come back the next weekend, and every weekend since. In fact, if I remember right, Paul has only missed about four Saturdays since his first visit.

Every Saturday, when Paul's truck would drive up our driveway, our dogs would bark with excitement, knowing they were in for a treat or two. Within a short period of time, Paul knew every dog's name and its story.

We had one dog that really stole Paul's heart. Her name was Irene. She was a large black and tan dog with a little white patch on her chest and paws—she was beautiful. We had rescued her because some creep in town had threatened to put a bullet in her head.

Every weekend, after Paul had made his rounds through the pens handing out treats, he would go back to Irene's pen and spend thirty or forty minutes talking to and playing with her. Irene loved him and would show it by giving him kisses and her full attention. Tony called it "puppy love."

After a few months had passed, Paul showed up at the rescue ranch one Saturday in October to discover that his best friend, Irene, had been adopted. Even though Paul was sad that she was gone, he was happy that she had finally found a home. And then a month later, the strangest thing happened.

On November 6, 1999, our mobile veterinarian, Dr. Kim Herndon, was at the rescue ranch to spay and neuter some of our dogs. Because I had overlooked getting Irene spayed, I had called the people who had adopted Irene and asked them to please bring her to the rescue ranch on that Saturday so we could get her spayed.

On that busy morning, Paul came out with his wife, Marty, so that Tony and I could finally meet her. We had a fun, short visit, and then Tony and Paul gave Marty the grand tour. While Marty was happily meeting our dogs and handing out her homemade garlic and cheese treats, Irene arrived.

Since Tony was temporarily out of pocket, I went over to the couple to greet and thank them for bringing Irene back so she could be spayed. As I talked to the couple, I found out that they had had several problems with Irene and the neighbors, and they were concerned for Irene's safety. They told me that the neighbors had threatened to poison Irene, and they didn't know what to do.

When Paul, Marty, and Tony returned from the pens, I walked over to tell Paul that Irene was here if he wanted to see her. Next, I told Marty about how much Paul and Irene had loved each other, and about how sad Paul had been when Irene had been adopted. Then I hollered over to the couple who had adopted Irene and told them that they needed to meet Paul, because he had been Irene's best friend and had wanted to adopt her, but couldn't.

The couple looked at one another, and then the man hollered back, "If you want her you can have her! We really don't want her anymore."

Marty looked at Paul, and then hollered, "We want her!"

With all of this hollering going on, I suggested that we go over to the truck to talk to the couple. After the introductions, the couple explained to Marty and Paul about the problem with their neighbors, and then they drove away—minus one dog.

All of us were in shock about the turn of events, but Paul seemed extremely happy about getting to adopt Irene.

When Dr. Kim came outside her mobile clinic to get Irene, she told us that she could not spay Irene, because Irene had just gone into heat;

we would have to wait at least two weeks before spaying her. That news didn't bother Marty or Paul at all. They told us they would go ahead and take Irene and get her spayed when it was time. After completing the adoption papers, Marty and Paul drove away with Irene happily sitting between them.

The next Saturday, when Paul came out to the rescue ranch, he reported that every male dog within a ten-mile radius had come to their house hoping to date Irene. He also told us that Irene was a fence jumper, and that he and Marty had to put up an electric wire. Then Paul told us that Irene had eaten herself out of a big, sturdy kennel that was guaranteed unbreakable. Next he said that they had taken Irene to their veterinarian, Dr. Masters, and Irene was now on some kind of "doggie Prozac" because she had issues with separation—she had eaten through the walls of their utility room and they could now see between the walls. And, lastly, Irene had destroyed all of the blinds in their home. He said the metal blinds were all bent and broken and the neighbors had complained about it.

By now, Tony, Paul, and I were starting to laugh uncontrollably, but Paul's report was not over yet. Paul told us, as Tony and I tried to stop laughing, but couldn't, that Irene had developed serious issues with squirrels and was now a tree climber. He showed us pictures of their backyard tree with Irene standing on a big limb about twenty feet high off the ground!

That did it for all of us; we laughed until there were tears in our eyes. As tears fell from Paul's face, he went on to tell us that he and Marty still wanted Irene, but they had decided to changed her name to Susie Irene. When Tony asked Paul how much the damages were, Paul replied, "Marty and I are calling her 'the Six Million Dollar Dog.'"

Every Saturday, Paul would come out with treats that Marty had cooked for our dogs and give us updates on Susie Irene's latest escapades. During the next nine months, Marty and Paul helped find homes for over two dozen of our dogs and, thankfully, none of those dogs was as destructive as Susie Irene!

On August 12, 2000, Marty and Paul brought out some friends of theirs who were interested in adopting a dog; their friends adopted Annie Oakley, and Paul and Marty adopted Gracie, a sweet, one-year-old Blue Lacey that was black.

The following Saturday, when Paul came out to the rescue ranch, he had great news to tell us—Gracie had cured Susie Irene! He told us that as soon as they got Gracie home, she and Susie Irene bonded instantly. And, for the first time since they had adopted Susie Irene, she had gone seven days without destroying anything.

After Paul had made his rounds in the pens, giving out treats and petting all of the dogs, the last thing he told us before leaving was that he and Marty had decided to ban Marty from coming to the rescue ranch, because every time that she did, a dog would come home with them.

On October 12, 2002, Paul arrived at the rescue ranch with a homemade housewarming present for our three-legged Pit Bull, Mama. Mama had stolen Paul's heart the day she arrived at the rescue ranch a couple of months earlier. She had been dumped in downtown Austin and left to die. A desperate woman had called the rescue ranch begging for our help. She told me that she had found a dog that was in terrible shape, but she could not afford to take the dog to a veterinarian. She then told me that the dog's back leg was dangling, and she thought it had been used as a fighting or bait dog.

I asked the woman if she could drive the dog to Kerrville, and her answer was yes. I told her that if she would do that we would take the dog, and then I gave her directions to Hoegemeyer Animal Clinic.

After our conversation, I called Susan Kelley at Hoegemeyer Animal Clinic and told her that a Pit Bull that was in pretty bad shape would be arriving in a few hours and asked her to please take care of her. Susan asked me what was the dog's name, and I said we will call her Mama.

Later that afternoon, Sara McGehee from Hoegemeyer's clinic called to tell me that Mama's leg had to be amputated and she was doing fine, but the doctors wanted to keep her for a few days before we could pick her up and bring her to the rescue ranch. That was good news, because we didn't have a pen for her.

The following day, Tony and Donnie Boner built Mama a beautiful pen nestled among the cedar trees. The next day, we picked up Mama and brought her to the rescue ranch. Besides stealing our hearts, she also stole Paul's.

Paul decided that he wanted to do something special for Mama, so he found some doghouse designs on the Internet and began building Mama's house. Every Saturday, Paul would come out to the rescue ranch and give us an update on his building project, bring treats for all of the dogs, and then leave a week's supply of giant rawhide bones for Mama to enjoy.

When Paul delivered Mama's mansion, it took Paul, Donnie, and Tony to carry it to her pen. Because it was so big and would not fit through the gate, Tony had to take down a portion of the fence to get it inside her pen. As soon as the chateau was on solid ground, Mama went inside to check it out and then returned to her front porch. Paul handed her a new rawhide bone, and she took it, laid down on her porch, and began chewing on it.

Paul told us that the floor plan was modeled after "the finest doghouses built." It had two bedrooms, a covered porch, and a lift-up roof! He told us that when a blue norther came through, Mama could go inside her house, take a left, and be shielded from the cold, and the lift-up roof would make it easy for Tony to clean.

When I asked Paul about the value of the house, so I could record his in-kind donation, he jokingly laughed and told me that it would have been $100 cheaper if they had just gone and bought the one that he had copied.

Time marched on. In September of 2005, Paul was at the rescue ranch when I drove up in the pickup with two Katrina rescue dogs, Marcia Ball, a beautiful Cocker mix, and Boudin, a wannabe Dachshund. I had just picked them up from Dr. Jonathan Brooke's River Hills Animal Clinic in Kerrville, because he had just treated them for heartworms. When Paul laid eyes on Marcia Ball, he was hooked. He helped me unload the two new evacuees into the front yard of my cabin before helping me feed and water them.

A few days later, after we had posted the Katrina dogs up on our website, Paul called and told me that he and Marty were thinking about adopting Marcia Ball, and he asked me to please e-mail them a few more pictures of her. That wasn't a problem, because Kinky had been over here playing with the dogs, and I had just taken a picture of him and Marcia Ball for his website.

After I e-mailed the Emersons, Paul called immediately. He told me that when Marty saw Marcia Ball in Kinky's arms, she wanted her. He asked me to hold on to Marcia Ball because he would pick her up on Saturday, just five days away.

Two days had passed when Marty called to ask me if she could drive out right then to adopt Marcia Ball because she couldn't wait till Saturday. My answer, of course, was yes.

When Marty arrived, she and Marcia Ball fell in love with each other. While Marty quickly filled out the adoption papers, she told me that she was changing Marcia Ball's name to Stella. I immediately got goose bumps and told her that the name was perfect, and I wished that I had come up with it.

As soon as Marty left the rescue ranch with Stella riding in her lap, I went over to the Lodge to see Kinky. When I told Kinky about the name change, he thought Stella was perfect. And then he teased me about being outdone for the very first time in naming our animals.

I hated to admit it—but he was so right.

After I left Kinky's Lodge, I went home and rewatched the video of *A Streetcar Named Desire*.

Mother Nature

Back in the spring of 1999, Tony and I met Linden Dokken, a friendly neighbor who lived in a trailer above the Sabinal River, about a mile south of Utopia. Linden, who went by the name Dok, was in his late sixties and was retired but made extra income by mowing ranches and drilling post holes with his tractor.

Dok's tractor was his pride and joy. Even though it was an old tractor,

Dok kept it spotlessly clean and well tuned. Not a day would pass when you didn't see Dok riding down the highway on his tractor, or else catch him in town at the Lost Maples Cafe, drinking coffee with the locals.

One day, Dok showed up at the rescue ranch on his tractor to formally introduce himself to us before offering to mow our ranch for free. He told us that he loved animals, especially dogs, and he just wanted to offer his services. The ranch badly needed mowing, so we took him up on his generous offer and let him mow away. That was the beginning of a long friendship.

Anytime that we needed holes drilled for fencing, Dok was the one that we called on. He was always on time, worked hard and fast, and would always give us a break in his price. In no time, Dok became a close friend of Tony's, and he would often come out to the rescue ranch just to help Tony with chores, visit our dogs, or go fishing in our huge stock tank.

In the evenings, Dok, and our good friend and neighbor Wayne Tacker, would often drop by to have a "fishing tournament" with Tony. The rules were simple—you won if you caught the first fish; you won if you caught the biggest fish; and you won if you caught the most fish. The only rule that we enforced was that you couldn't keep the fish or eat it—you had to release it back to the stock tank, which they abided by.

On August 8, 2000, late in the afternoon, Dok came out to the rescue ranch in his pickup to visit with Tony. After helping Tony feed the dogs, spot clean the pens, and give out doggie treats, they had a serious conversation at the picnic table.

I was inside doing paperwork, when Tony came inside the trailer to tell me that Dok wanted to know if he could adopt Maxwell Smart. He said that Dok had told him that he was really lonely, and had cried. He said that Dok really liked Max and thought that he, one of our biggest, smartest black Labs, would be good company for him. I immediately wrote up the adoption papers, and Tony and I went outside to adopt Max to Dok.

Dok signed the adoption papers excitedly, and when Tony walked up with Max on a leash, Dok took the leash from Tony, with tears trickling down from his eyes. Max then walked over to Dok's side and licked his hand. Dok smiled at the two of us as he hugged Max, while promising him that he would give him a great home. Then they left in Dok's truck with Max sitting happily in the passenger seat. They looked liked two old friends as they drove away.

From that point on, every time that we saw Dok, Max was always with him; they had become inseparable. And every time that we ran into Dok, he would go on and on about Max being the smartest and greatest dog that he had ever had. In fact, Max even got to sleep with him on the bed—something that Dok had never allowed any dog to do before.

In the summer of 2002, after we had moved the rescue ranch over to Echo Hill Ranch, the Hill Country was besieged with rainstorms for over thirty days. At the rescue ranch, by the end of the thirty days, we had received over thirty-five inches of rain in just one month, as had the rest of the Hill Country.

During our ten days and ten nights of constant rain, Tony rescued two horses that had gotten themselves stuck in a landslide that had covered them up to the tops of their hips. The giant cliff behind the rescue ranch began having more and more landslides that miraculously always seemed to stop at the back of our dog pens, and we would be landlocked at least once or twice a week at the rescue ranch because of the flooding creeks.

When the creeks would go down, Kinky, Tony, and I would hightail it together to Kerrville to get food and any supplies we needed, before the next storm would arrive. It was a real mess, to say the least. In fact, the Hill Country was flooding so badly that Tony's doublewide trailer in Utopia was washed away and was last seen going down the Sabinal River headed for Sabinal, but it never arrived—it was a total loss.

We didn't think things could get any worse until we received a phone call from the Sheriff in Uvalde County. Early afternoon on July 2, 2002, the Sheriff called us to tell us that our good friend Dok had drowned. He told Tony that Dok had been drinking coffee at the Lost Maples Cafe with his friends and owners of the cafe, Rusty and Tacy Redden, when the Sabinal River went out of its banks. Dok told Tacy and Rusty that he needed to get home. Even though the Reddens begged Dok not to go, Dok left the cafe and headed home on his tractor in the torrential rain. He was just barely out of town when a neighbor saw Dok and his tractor get washed away by the rushing waters—never to be seen again.

The Sheriff knew that Dok was a good friend of ours and asked Tony if he knew how to get in touch with Dok's son, Curtis. Tony gave the Sheriff Curtis's phone number and then hung up the phone.

Tony cried as he told me about what had happened to Dok.

Later that day, we found out that Dok's trailer had also been washed away by the flood. After a couple of days had passed, Tony and I figured out why Dok had ignored the advice from his friends to stay at the cafe and chose to risk his life to get to his trailer—he had gone to the trailer to rescue his best friend, Max.

Dok's funeral was held in Utopia, and Tony and I were unable to attend it because we were flooded in.

Couch Potato

I have been best friends with Maribeth Couch since the day I left Austin and moved to Utopia, Texas, back in 1995. Being a typical Virgo, Maribeth more or less took me under her wing (Virgos are mothering types) when I was "the new kid in town" (the town being Utopia, and I being forty-three).

When we decided to start the rescue ranch, Maribeth's support and hard work in the community made it much easier for us to get the rescue ranch up and running. In other words, she was gung ho—big time! After many months of having her help as a volunteer, we decided that we needed to hire someone part-time. So we hired her.

With Tony being a Leo, Maribeth being a Virgo, and me being a Libra, the combination of our three signs worked out beautifully. If Tony wasn't borrowing Maribeth off of me or me borrowing her from Tony, it was the three of us working together.

Through the years Maribeth has often made runs to the San Antonio airport to ship a dog out or to pick one up, or else she has run up to

Kerrville to take a dog to the vet or to pick one up. If a job needed doing, she did it and she did it right.

When we had decided to move the rescue ranch to Kinky's family ranch in Medina, Maribeth played a significant part in helping build pens, moving animals, and keeping me sane throughout the ordeal.

A few years back, a friend of Kinky's fell on some hard times and was unable to take proper care of his Macaw. After several discussions we decided that we would help Kinky's friend and take his Macaw, Tim McCaw, and find him a home as soon as possible. I was nervous about taking the responsibility of caring for the beautiful bird, since the last time that I had had a bird, a gray Senegal Parrot that I named Elvis back in 1992, he had died within a week of being in my care.

In my defense, I had purchased Elvis from a disreputable bird dealer up in Austin, and he had sold Elvis to me knowing full well that he was sick. Before I left the man's aviary he told me to play with Elvis daily and to spend as much time as possible letting him get to know me.

The first four days that I had Elvis, he became calmer and gentler every day. On the fifth morning I awoke to discover that he was tilting far over to the right and seemed sick. I put him in a shoe box and rushed him to the best bird doctor in Austin. I went to work and anxiously waited for three hours to find out Elvis's diagnosis.

When this highly recommended but wacky bird doctor called me, he told me that Elvis was sicker than a dog but was in stable condition, sleeping in a little bed and being fed intravenously. He told me that Elvis might not make it through the night.

The following morning the bird vet called to tell me that Elvis had left the building; in other words, he was dead. I was heartbroken even though the vet had reassured me that it wasn't my fault. He had done an autopsy, and the parrot had been sick for a very long time.

Before hanging up the phone, the vet asked me what I wanted him to do with Elvis's body. He told me I had two options: one, to cremate him, or two, to bury him at the vet's privately owned pet cemetery. I would have to come and pick out a coffin before Elvis could be properly buried. The cost for the cremation or burial was a minimum of two hundred dollars!

I was so mad. I told him to just put Elvis back in the shoe box and dispose of him; Elvis didn't care—he was dead! The creepy vet then told me that he could not do that, and I must pick one of his burial plans.

I calmly asked the vet how much I owed him for Elvis, and he told me the amount was three hundred dollars. In a matter-of-fact voice, I told the vet that if he wanted me to pay him his three hundred dollars, he needed to dispose of Elvis. There was a long silence on the line. Finally, the vet said, "Yes, ma'am." And then we hung up on each other. And that is why I was hesitant about caring for this beautiful Macaw parrot, Tim McCaw.

I called Maribeth to tell her about the rescue ranch getting Tim McCaw in a week or so, and, before I could finish my sentence, she had already read my mind and asked if she could adopt him. It was a perfect match, because Maribeth and her husband, T-Bone, loved birds and always had all kinds of birds that they took care of. And, on top of that, they had always wanted a Macaw. Maribeth, once again, to the rescue.

Last year, T-Bone Couch became really ill and was bedridden. Maribeth had to do everything for him, so she gave him a little bell to ring when he needed her. As the days, weeks, and months passed, the little bell system worked out great. When T-Bone needed something he would ring the bell, wait a few seconds, and then holler from their bedroom, "Maribeth?"

One evening, Maribeth was in the kitchen when she heard T-Bone holler from the bedroom, "Maribeth?" She dropped what she was doing and went to check on him. When she came inside the bedroom, T-Bone was reading a book. She asked him what he wanted and he told her nothing.

Maribeth went back to the kitchen, and ten minutes later, T-Bone called out her name. Once again, Maribeth went straight to the bedroom and asked T-Bone what he wanted, and his answer was the same, "nothing."

So Maribeth returned to the kitchen, and a few minutes passed when her husband called her name again. For the third time, she stopped what she was doing and went to T-Bone. She asked him what he wanted and for the third time it was the same. Maribeth then asked him why he kept calling her, and why he wasn't ringing the bell.

He looked at her like she was crazy, and she returned the same stare. He hadn't called her; in fact, he swore he had never called her.

Maribeth had an idea, so she went into the living room, sat down, and waited on the couch to confirm her suspicion. Several minutes passed, and then Tim McCaw looked right at her and said in T-Bone's voice, "Maribeth?"

Some Like It Hot!

I t was hotter than hot on July 30, 2002, and on that day, it even got hotter!

At 11:55, the phone rang at the rescue ranch; as everyone who knows me knows, I screen all calls and never pick up the phone, but for some reason I answered this call—and thank goodness I did.

A man with a pleasant voice introduced himself to me as Jerry Agiewich and told me that he was a former member of the Humane Society of Williamson County—a director, to be exact. He and his wife, Sue, wanted to develop a line of salsas for their stores, Truly Texas, to benefit the rescue ranch!

Our rescue ranch gets all kinds of calls like this, but Jerry somehow was different; he really impressed me. He wasn't pushy at all, and, by the time we had finished our conversation, I told him that I liked his idea but would have to run it by Kinky first. As soon as I had hung up the phone, I called Kinky and told him about Jerry's proposition. Kinky invited me over to the Lodge to discuss it further. I told Kinky that I thought Jerry sounded like a really nice man and asked Kinky to call him.

Following Kinky's conversation with Jerry, Kinky discovered that he and Jerry had a lot in common, besides their love for animals. For instance, they were the same age, had both been born in Chicago, and were Jewish, to top it off! Besides sharing the common ground with him, Kinky liked him, and he and Jerry made a deal. The wheels were set in motion.

On August 7th, Jerry drove down from Georgetown to see the rescue ranch and to meet us. Unfortunately, Kinky was out of town, but we had a very nice meeting and Jerry liked what he saw. Nine days later, I met up with Jerry and Liz and Jim Cravotta at Chili's in Fredericksburg for lunch and an informal business meeting. Before our power lunch was over, Jerry had hired Liz as the official artist, and, between the four of us making wisecracks, Jerry had decided on the names for the four salsas.

The salsas are under the name "Kinky Friedman's Private Stock," and they are absolutely delicious! I, like many others, have wondered how Jerry came up with the four tasty, award-winning recipes, but Jerry won't tell me—it's a secret. However, I do know that he has the recipes safely tucked away, hidden in an underground, waterproof safe located somewhere in Williamson County.

Even though I don't have the recipes, I can tell you that the Pickin' & Grinnin' salsa has peaches in it; the Politically Correct Salsa & Dip is perfect; Lucky's Lone Star Caviar, named after our three-legged cat, has black-eyed peas in it; and the Black Hat Edition, my personal favorite, is loaded with black beans and corn.

It is a win/win situation for everyone! The person who purchases these super-fine salsas is getting their money's worth in flavor and quality, and, as they enjoy their salsa and dip, our animals at the rescue ranch are benefiting as well. Quite simply, it is brilliant: the more you eat, the better our animals can eat, sleep, and be merry!

Kinky's Private Stock salsas have been flying off of the grocery shelves, all over the United States, for years now, and the answer to the question that many have asked is: no, Kinky has never received one red cent from the sale of these salsas; his proceeds go directly to the rescue ranch to help the animals. And, may I note here, this is just one more example as to why the rescue ranch considers Kinky to be our Gandhi-like figure.

As for Jerry and Sue Agiewich, who truly put their time and money into this labor of love, which they call their "financial pleasure project," benefiting the Utopia Animal Rescue Ranch—there are no words that can ever thank them enough!

For anyone interested in helping out our rescue ranch by purchasing these fine salsas but can't find them at their local supermarket, please go to: www.kinkysprivatestock.com.

Kindred Spirits

In June 2003, our friends Jim and Liz Cravotta called us about their dear friends Bill and Barbara Kindred, both of whom were dying of cancer, without much time left for either of them. Bill and Barbara had two horses that they had been desperately trying to find loving homes for, but with no luck. Jim and Liz made a call to us to see if we could help, and our answer was yes.

An hour later, Tony and I were at the Cravotta's ranch in Center Point, Texas. Jim and Liz then took us over to the Kindred's ranch, where we met Barbara and had a long, sad talk. Unfortunately, Bill wasn't feeling well that afternoon, so we never had the opportunity to meet him. After all was said and done that day, Barbara gave Tony and me their two horses, which, in turn, we promised never to sell or separate.

Before leaving the Kindred Ranch, Barbara introduced us to our horses. Girls first: I met my horse, By Day, an eighteen-year-old wild mustang mare, out of Arizona, who was captured when she was under six months of age and then hand-raised and trained by Bill Kindred. I fell in love with her immediately.

It was now Tony's turn to meet his horse, Serenity, By Day's eight-year-old son, who was half wild mustang and half quarter horse. (Question: Half wild and half quarter? Does that make him five-eighths of a horse?) Tony and Serenity checked each other out and quickly bonded after Tony fed him an apple.

One week later, the horses arrived at the ranch. Before they were unloaded by Jim Cravotta and Jeanie Parker, I renamed my horse Seabiscuit and Tony's horse Trigger.

On July 23, 2003, the Cravottas called and informed us that Bill Kindred had passed away and that Barb's passing would be very soon. Barbara had asked Jim and Liz to ask us if we could help her one last time. She had no luck trying to find homes for her and Bill's two aging Cocker Spaniels and wanted to know if we could take them, too.

On the morning of July 25, 2003, Jim and Liz came out to the rescue ranch to deliver the Kindred's Cockers—Harold and Maude! They were absolutely adorable. Harold, the blonde one, was fifteen years old, and Maude (Maudie) was a jet-black, thirteen-years-young Cocker. The dogs also came along with a surprise $1,000 check from Barbara to sponsor a pen in loving memory of her husband, Bill Kindred. Harold and Maude fit right in, even though their hearts had been broken. Everyone at the ranch fell in love with them.

October 23, 2003, Harold passed away. Tony found him inside his doghouse, which was being carefully guarded by Maudie. Tony and Ben Welch dug him a grave under an old oak tree that had shaded his and Maudie's pen. Burying Harold was for sure one of our saddest and worst days at the rescue ranch.

Maude was all alone now. She had lost everyone that she had loved. A couple of days after Harold's passing, we decided to give Maudie a new roommate, hoping that would cheer her up. We chose Dottie West, a sweet Dalmatian who had been abused.

We decided that the best way to introduce them was to have them meet on mutual ground outside of the rescue ranch. Tony put a leash on Dottie and I put a leash on Maudie, and we introduced them near the swimming hole on Echo Hill Ranch. The two ladies sniffed each other from top to bottom, and then we went for a short walk through the woods. By the time the walk was over we felt it was safe to take them back to the rescue ranch and put them in Maudie's pen. With our fingers crossed, and a few silent prayers, we released them in the pen and stepped outside. Dottie trotted around her new pen checking things out as Maudie sat inside her doghouse at the front door as if claiming it as hers. Dottie didn't seem to mind and quickly settled down in Harold's old house. The two of them soon became the best of friends and seemed to enjoy each other's company.

Winter came and passed. By early spring, Maudie had congenital heart failure. She was becoming more and more frail every day and spent most of her time in her doghouse. Even though she was taking three to four pills a day for all of her ailments, she still seemed to be happy, always greeting us with the wagging tail that didn't exist.

On May 20, 2004, at exactly 3:49 p.m., our ranch received a very special phone call from some kindred spirits! I still get goose bumps when I think of it.

I had just finished helping Tony feed all of the dogs and was on my way up the steps into the trailer. As I walked inside, I heard a call coming in on the answering machine: "Hello, this is Susan. My husband and I want to adopt Harold and Maude, but we can't find Harold's picture on your website. Please call us. . . ."

I was in shock. I picked up the phone.

"Hello, this is Nancy. I just walked in," I said. "You want to adopt Harold and Maude?"

"Yes, but we can't find Harold's picture. Your website says that they have to go together."

"Oh, dear. I must've forgotten to change that," I said. "Unfortunately, Harold passed away, but Maudie sure does need a home. Although she is awfully frail and on all kinds of medications."

"That's fine. We want her, anyway. Michael and I like taking care of the old ones." Susan said. "We find it very rewarding!"

"She has congenital heart failure," I added, hoping not to discourage her.

"Not a problem," Susan said. "Michael and I work out of our house and are always home. We have dog beds in every room and food bowls scattered all over the house. Can we have her? Please say yes."

"Susan, this is fantastic! Yes, of course, you can have her! Good grief, this is unbelievable!"

Susan put her husband on the phone and I gave him the driving directions to our rescue ranch.

I phoned Kinky to tell him the great news. He was off in Mexico City at the time, attending a friend's wedding, but I was sure that he would want to know.

We first said our *holas* to each other, and then I told him what was going on.

"Maude?" Kinky asked. "They want Maudie?"

"Yes, Kinky! They are wonderful people and are coming out tomorrow to pick her up!"

"Nance, did you tell them about her heart condition and all the pills?"

"Yes, Kinky. I told them everything and they still want her! I am so excited for her!"

"Be sure to show them Louise," Kinky added. "She's old, too, and maybe they will want her also."

"I will."

"This is great news," Kinky said. "Please give them my best and thank them for me. I'm having a great time down here, but I wish that I could be there to send our Maudie off."

"Kinky, this is one of the greatest adoptions that we have ever had! Just think! Maudie is fixing to spend the rest of her life in the lap of luxury and be surrounded in love!"

"I know," Kinky said. "Just when you think there are no good people left in this world—people like them show up."

Kinky and I then said our *adioses.*

On May 21, 2004, Susan and Michael arrived at the ranch around five o'clock in the evening. It was love at first sight; they instantly fell in love with Maude—and she with them—and we with them! As Susan and Michael drove away with Maudie happily sitting in their back seat, I thanked God that there were still kindred spirits like them out there. As Tony and I waved good-bye to Maudie as they drove away, we both teared up and were unable to speak for a couple of minutes.

The next morning we took Dottie West for another walk and introduced her to her new roommate, Monica Lewinsky, a medium-sized red dog with wiry hair. And they got along just fine.

Three days later, on May 24, 2003, Susan called to give us an update on Maude. We talked for over ten minutes and found out that Maude was doing great in her new home and everything was working out splendidly. Maudie had bonded with them before they had even reached Austin, and she loved their furniture—especially when she could cuddle with them on the couch. Susan also thanked me over and over again for letting them adopt her, and all I could do, between the tears, was to thank them for who they were and what they had done for our Maudie.

Pet of the Week

August 12, 2003, on a Tuesday afternoon, Kinky brought his friends Steve Alex and Harley Belew over to the rescue ranch for a tour and a visit. Little did we know at the time how important that visit was going to be for the animals at our rescue ranch.

Kinky, Tony, and I had a lot of fun that day visiting with Steve and Harley. They were absolutely hilarious and full of the funniest stories that we had ever heard.

Harley impressed me right off the bat, when he told me he was born and raised in Fort Worth—as was I. I've never met anyone from Fort Worth that I didn't like, and I often get teased about my feelings for Fort Worth, by Kinky and Tony.

Steve impressed me, too, when he told me that he also had lived in Fort Worth and loved that city, but what especially impressed me about him was he took over my kitchen and began cooking fifty cheese and garlic quesadillas to feed to the dogs outside. While Steve was turning out one quesadilla after another, Harley and I had a long conversation about growing up in Cowtown before Kinky diverted our attention back to the subject of the rescue ranch. When the quesadillas were ready to be served, we all went out to the pens to pass them out to our fifty dogs.

Just before Tony was bitten on the finger by an overly anxious dog waiting for his quesadilla to be served, Steve said, "What can we do to help the rescue ranch?"

"Ouch!" Tony said, as he stared at his bleeding finger.

"Are you okay?" Kinky asked Tony.

"Kinky, Steve and I would really like to help the rescue ranch out," Harley said. "What do y'all think about us doing a weekly phone-in interview and talk about the rescue ranch?"

"I'm fine, but I had better get to the trailer and put some medicine on it," Tony said.

"That would be fantastic!" Kinky remarked, to both Tony and Harley.

"How about Cousin Nancy doing the show?" Steve asked, as he turned and looked at me. "Would you like to do about a ten-minute talk once a week on our show?"

"Sure," I answered. "When?"

"Let's do it every Monday morning at 7:10," Harley said. "We've got a spot open for that time frame in the morning."

Before leaving the rescue ranch that day, Steve and Harley traded business cards with us. They told me to give them a call, and we would set the wheels in motion to get my call-in deal started.

Following Harley and Steve's departure, Tony complained about his sore finger, and I whined about my back starting to ache. Kinky laughed and said, "Cousin Nancy, your back is hurting because you laughed too much today!"

Each weekday morning, between the hours of six and nine, Harley and Steve do the most hilarious, entertaining show on KRVL 94.3, a Hill Country Radio Network, called the "Steve & Harley Show." It is the best morning radio show heard in the Texas Hill Country simply because Steve and Harley are intelligent, funny, and entertaining.

On Monday, September 8, 2003, at ten minutes past seven o'clock in the morning, I called Steve and Harley for the very first time to discuss the rescue ranch. Having never done a radio show, I was a nervous wreck, hoping that I wouldn't come off sounding like a moron and making the rescue ranch look bad.

Before going on the air live, I told Steve and Harley about my concerns, and they told me to relax and just pretend that I was just talking to them—not the entire Hill Country.

Well, that was easier said than done, but thanks to Harley and Steve for walking me through it, it went pretty well.

Tootsie, a small, black wannabe Dachshund, was the first to be "Steve & Harley's Pet of the Week!" We talked about her and the rescue ranch, and I answered a lot of their questions. The three of us also did a lot of laughing. It lasted for nearly ten minutes.

When I got off the air, Tony came inside the trailer. Since we can't pick up KRVL's signal inside our metal trailer, I had asked Tony to go out and sit in the pickup, and record the show, so I could critique myself afterward and do a better show next week. When I asked Tony how I did, he said, "It was good. You sounded like Gabby Hayes on helium."

Later that afternoon, Tootsie got adopted to a great home by one of Steve and Harley's listeners!

One of the funniest times on their show was on December 22, 2003; Steve and Harley, off the air, had told me that they had some extra air time to fill, so we would be talking a little longer than usual.

We started off talking about Big Foot and Kate being the "Steve & Harley's Pet of the Week." Kate and her brother, Big Foot, were our two biggest dogs at the rescue ranch. They weighed over a hundred and thirty pounds each, and that's when Harley and Steve began teasing me and saying things like, "Folks, if you go out to the rescue ranch and you see two gigantic dogs wearing tires around their necks instead of collars—that'll be Kate and Big Foot."

Here I am on the radio, trying to get someone to adopt these two dogs, and Steve and Harley wouldn't quit making jokes about them and cracking me up.

"Cousin Nancy, tell us, how many cows do they eat per day?" they asked. "Do you and Tony ride them around on Kinky's ranch? We hope that they are house trained, because it would sure be awful if they had an accident inside and put a huge hole in the middle of someone's trailer."

I was laughing so hard, I had tears in my eyes.

"Kate and Big Foot are two of the sweetest dogs that we have ever had," I said, trying not to laugh.

"Have they ever killed anything?" Harley asked.

"Yes," I answered. "Last week, Kate jumped out of her pen and fought a giant wild hog and killed it. The next morning Tony had to take her to Hoegemeyer Animal Clinic because the hog had eaten off the side of her muzzle, and she required over fifty stitches, but . . ."

"Cousin Nancy, stop!" they said, jokingly. "We're trying to help you get these dogs a home, and you're telling us she killed a wild hog? What else have they killed?"

"Maybe a porcupine," I said. "That was a real mess! They had these quills all over their faces and bodies and Tony had to take them to Hoegemeyer Animal Clinic to get the quills removed and . . ."

After several more funny remarks from Steve and Harley they changed the subject. They began taking turns reading out celebrities' birthdays for that day and making comments.

"Can you believe that today is Barbara Billingsley's birthday and she is eighty-one years old?" Steve said.

"Really? She was the woman who played June Cleaver on the *Leave It to Beaver* show," Harley commented.

"Well, how old is the Beaver?" I asked.

Steve and Harley then broke out laughing hysterically. Shortly after that we ended our conversation; we had filled the extra air time.

Doing the weekly morning shows with them has been a blast for me, and, thanks to Steve and Harley, our adoption rate has since skyrocketed!

Kinky, Tony, and I will never be able to thank them enough for all that they have done to help our animals and the rescue ranch. We count them as friends, and our gates will always be open for them.

Brian's Story

Brian Alstott has been a major player in helping out the rescue ranch over the years. Tony and I first met him back in 1996, while I was running Kinky's first fan club, the Kinky Friedman Crime Club, which ended up not being a financial success for Kinky or me.

Brian was living up in Dallas at the time and had ordered some merchandise from me, and he called to check on his order. During our conversation I invited him to come to Utopia and promised to give him a tour of the Texas Hill Country, which included taking him to meet Kinky over in Medina.

Brian took me up on my offer and a few weeks later drove down from Big D to my ranch. After meeting Tony, Brian and I took off in my old 1980 pickup, Trigger, headed for Kerrville and then Kinky's.

It took about ten minutes in Kerrville to drive Brian around the town. He was very impressed with the famous Butt-Holdsworth Library, Wal-Mart, and Wolfmueller's Books, where we stopped so he could empty his pockets on Kinky memorabilia and a few of his books. Our next stop was Joe's Jefferson Street Cafe, where they were having some kind of a celebration. Brian and I celebrated for about as long as it took to drink a glass of wine, and then we headed for Echo Hill Ranch.

Unfortunately, Kinky was out of town, but he had given me permission to bring Brian over for a tour of the ranch and the Lodge. Even though Brian was disappointed about not getting to meet Kinky, he was excited about getting to see the famous ranch.

Since that day Brian has become the best of friends with Kinky, Tony, and me. But being best friends with Kinky does require a little work, as Brian soon found out.

The first time that I took Brian over to meet Kinky, Kinky already had a job for him to do. Kinky had a flat tire, and Brian's job was to help him change the tire and fix the flat. To most people, changing a tire is no big deal, but not in this case. It ended up taking all three of us.

First off, Kinky's jack was broken. Next, we tried my jack, which not only weighed about a ton but also had a very important part missing. Brian then got his jack, but it was too short. Putting our three heads together it was decided that we would stack some walking stones until the jack was high enough to raise Kinky's vehicle. To Kinky's and my amazement, it worked. We stood by and watched as Brian jacked up the car, pulled the tire, and then replaced it with one of those donut tires. Kinky was delighted!

Brian's next visit to Kinky's required heavy lifting. A norther was headed our direction and Kinky asked Brian and me to help him get all of his plants inside so they wouldn't freeze. To Kinky's and my amazement again, Brian successfully carried in twenty-two plants—two small, eight medium, nine large, and three gigantic fifty-five pound pots—in under five minutes. Kinky was delighted again!

The next visit was really interesting. Brian brought his friend Larry Preston, from Oregon, with us over to meet Kinky. There was no job for Brian, so we just drank coffee and visited while Kinky opened up his mail. Kinky opened up a letter and told us that someone had sent him a royalty check for three dollars and twelve cents—payable to Frank Zappa! All of us started laughing, and Kinky wondered who he should forward the check to.

"Moon Unit!" all of us replied.

"Maybe I should frame it?" Kinky asked.

Then the phone rang and it was Dwight Yoakam. Kinky took the call, told him about the check, and asked Dwight what he thought he should do with it. Whatever Dwight said, Kinky roared with laughter, but he never told us Dwight's advice.

When Kinky, Tony, and I started the rescue ranch, Brian was one of the first to support us. The rescue ranch had so little money in the beginning that we used Tony's and my pickup, Trigger, my old computer and old fax machine, etc., because the rescue ranch could not afford anything else. Trigger made so many trips to the veterinarian's office in Kerrville, sixty miles away, that by January we had to park it and let the grass grow around it. Fortunately, Tom Friedman, Kinky's father, loaned us the use of his Echo Hill truck so we could keep going.

My ancient 1993 Mac computer, which I loved, was becoming so overloaded with my stuff and the ranch stuff that I'd say a prayer every time that I would boot it up. One Saturday, Tony and I had gone to town to get something, and when we returned to the ranch Brian was sitting outside the trailer waiting for us. The three of us went inside the trailer and sat down to visit. Then Brian started asking me weird questions like: "Have you got any bumper stickers? What kind of ink cartridge do you use?" and so on.

Finally, he asked me some question which caused me to get up and go back into my office to bring him something. When I brought whatever it was back he looked stunned!

"What?" I asked.

"Didn't you see it?" Brian asked.

"What?" I asked. "See what?"

Brian laughed and said, "The big box sitting in the middle of your office!"

With that said, Tony went back to my office and returned with a huge box and a big smile on his face.

Brian had brought a brand new iMac for the rescue ranch! He had snuck into my office while we had run to town. And, because I am as blind as a bat, I never even noticed it when he sent me to the office. In fact, I actually walked around it and hadn't even noticed it!

Brian's computer has been a lifesaver for the rescue ranch, and since then he has showed up with a hi-tech fax/copy/printer machine. In other words, he single-handedly equipped the rescue ranch office with all state-of-the-art equipment.

When my mother passed away, he sent a huge donation to the rescue ranch, made in loving memory of her. Then when Tom Friedman passed, Brian sent another giant donation to us, made in his loving memory.

Brian was also responsible for getting Hank, Jr., one of our cutest rescued dogs, adopted to his friends Mark and Denise Stevens. And if that hasn't been enough, when his mother sadly passed away in the spring of 2004, he sent the rescue ranch another large amount of money to sponsor a pen made in loving memory of her from Brian, his brother, and his sister, Marleen. He requested that his mother's sign read "Kathleen's Corner," because she was a great woman and an avid animal lover, and was loved so much.

Besides being a dear friend to all of us, Brian has helped out the rescue ranch so many times that it isn't even funny, and we love him.

Knock, Knock, Knocking On

Ben Welch, an Aquarian, has been a godsend to the rescue ranch even though he is Uranus-ruled. He is pushing thirty years and lives up in Austin, Texas. For the past three years, Ben has been driving down weekly to our rescue ranch to help us out by doing whatever is needed.

In Austin, Ben is a chocolatier by day and an enterprising entrepreneur by night, selling the designer T-shirts he designs. He is multi-talented, and it seems that there is nothing that Ben cannot do or fix.

As a child, Ben and his family had numerous family dogs, but none were just his. Knowing that Ben wanted to have his very own dog, his parents, Rob and Karen Welch, gave him permission when he turned sixteen to have one.

Ben knew exactly what kind of dog he wanted and immediately went and found one. It was a purple (red and blue mixed) Heeler pup that he named Newt. He and Newt were always together; they were inseparable—buddies for life.

Being a Heeler, Newt became very protective of Ben. In fact, one time when Ben's mother was trying to wake Ben up for school, Newt gently grabbed her nose, and just held it between his teeth, until Ben woke up and told him to quit. Later that very same day, when Ben came home from school, he found a mysterious present wrapped up in pretty paper sitting on the kitchen table with his name on it. The card on the gift box read: "For Ben, from Anonymous." It was an alarm clock.

A couple of years later, Newt accompanied Ben off to college, at Texas Tech, where he helped Ben make it through the partying nights and ultimately graduation.

For the past years that Ben has been coming down to work at the rescue ranch Newt was always with him. Even though Newt was getting long in the teeth, he got along great with all of "the Friedmans" (Kinky's five dogs), as well as any other visiting dogs. During this time the only person that Newt ever bit was one of Kinky's and our dear friends, Nelda Cabiness, and it wasn't on her nose.

In September 2003, Ben's heart was broken—Newt had been diagnosed with cancer, and he was full of tumors. After several visits to the veterinarian, the doctor told Ben that Newt was in pain and that there was nothing more that could be done for his eleven-year-old best friend. The veterinarian recommended euthanasia but told Ben that he must be the one to make the final call.

Ben made the decision. As he cried with Newt in his arms, Newt was gently put down by a lethal injection.

As soon as Ben told Kinky, Kinky called us to tell us the bad news. He told us that Ben was really depressed about losing Newt and was going to have Newt cremated. The next week, when Ben came down to work, he seemed changed. Instead of being his outgoing self, he was quiet and had little to say. Kinky, Tony, and I were frustrated because we did not know what we could do to get Ben out of his depression.

About a month after Newt had died, Kinky called to tell me that he wanted to donate one thousand dollars to sponsor a pen in Newt's name to honor him. He told me that if Ben asked me who had made the donation I was to tell him that the donor had asked to remain anonymous (until I wrote this book).

Well, Ben may have been depressed, but he sure wasn't stupid. When I told Ben about the plaque that was being made in honor of Newt, he knew exactly who had done it, even though Kinky denied it when Ben had asked him about it.

As the months passed, Ben slowly returned to being the old Ben that we all loved. The day that Jim and Liz Cravotta delivered Newt's plaque to the rescue ranch Ben was delighted when he saw it and was anxious to hang it. The pen that Ben chose to hang Newt's sign on was the last pen on the east side of the rescue ranch, where Rosie and Reba McIntyre resided. The wooden plaque read: "Newt's Friends."

In late January 2004, Kinky called and requested that the three of us have a meeting concerning a dog. At our meeting, as we sipped Kinky's Kona coffee, he asked us if we remembered the two young women from California who had recently visited us at the rescue ranch. We told Kinky that we didn't remember them, because we have so many visitors out at the ranch.

Wanting to help jog our memories, Kinky went on to tell us that they were the ones who had mud-wrestled with his good friend John McCall at a charity event. Unfortunately, that information still didn't ring any bells with us. Kinky gave up trying to enlighten us about the mystery women, so he told us that they were now up in Austin vacationing.

Tony and I were dumbfounded as to why we needed to know all of this information about two women that we couldn't remember, and we wondered why Kinky felt it was so important to update us about their journey.

Finally, Kinky put it in a nutshell. The wandering women had visited the Austin pound the day before and that was why we were having this "morning meeting of the minds."

Kinky told us that there was a beautiful, young, female Pit Bull on death row, at the pound, who only had a few days left to live before it would be killed. The nomadic gals had told Kinky that the dog was harmless, and as sweet as she could be, and they had asked him to please help them rescue this young dog. They also told Kinky that they would handle the adoption up there and get the dog to our rescue ranch if he would just say yes. He told them that he would get back to them after talking to us about it.

When Kinky's coffee pot was empty, our meeting was adjourned. The three of us had decided to let the Pit Bull come to our rescue ranch even though we were full and had no space available, which meant that Tony would have to build a new pen. Before we left the Lodge, Kinky phoned the traveling vagabonds to tell them the good news. The wheels were now set in motion.

On January 28, 2004, the rescue ranch received a call from one of the California girls. They had adopted the Pit Bull and had kept it at their hotel, and they were now ready to have their friend from Austin drive the dog out to the rescue ranch later that afternoon. I was disappointed that the women weren't delivering the dog, because I wanted to meet them to see if I could remember them.

Thank goodness Ben was working at the rescue ranch that day, helping Tony build the new dog pen for the Pit Bull. When I told them that the Pit Bull was coming in, they told me the pen was finished and ready to receive.

At two o'clock, my dogs inside the trailer began barking. I looked out the window and saw someone in a car driving slowly up to the trailer. Ben and Tony were following right behind the car in our pickup. I stepped outside onto the porch and went to greet the visitors who had parked down by the pig pen. Before I had made it to the car a young woman had gotten out with the Pit Bull on a leash and began talking to Tony and Ben.

The Pit Bull was absolutely beautiful! She was solid white with a big, blue, pancake-sized patch around her left eye. She reminded me of the dog in the '50s TV show *The Little Rascals*.

As I walked up to greet the woman, and to meet this good-looking dog, I decided on what her new name would be. I said, "Her name is Valentine!"

"No," Ben said, wearing a big grin on his face, while holding the dog in his arms. "Her name is Valerie and I want her! She's mine!"

Talk about happy—I didn't know who was the happiest!

After taking care of the paperwork, the young girl drove away, and I rushed inside the trailer to call Kinky. After learning about Valentine, aka Valerie, Kinky was thrilled to hear that Ben had adopted her on the spot. That was a good day for all of us.

Since that day, Ben and Valerie have been inseparable. She goes everywhere with Ben and is one of the sweetest dogs I have ever known. There is not one mean bone in her body, and she has never bitten or growled at anyone, no matter how provoked. Ben has spoiled her rotten, and she even sleeps on the bed with him.

There is still only one problem that I have with Ben: he won't let me put a baby-pink collar on Valerie. I guess it has something to do with him being ruled by Uranus—he can't help it.

PART FIVE

Head 'Em Up and
Move 'Em Out

Roy, Gabby, &
Little Jewford

My writing cabin

Little Jewford

By Day with Jim &
Liz Cravotta

Kinky with Imus in the
Morning

June and Louise—best
friends

Our sign by Liz Cravotta

Roy Rogers

Looking for Land in All the Wrong Places

In the fall of 2001, Kinky, Tony, and I decided that the rescue ranch had outgrown itself, and we needed to move it to a bigger ranch. On several occasions, Kinky and I spent a full day with area realtors looking at land to possibly buy for the rescue ranch. It ended up being a waste of our time. Every ranch that we looked at wasn't good enough for one reason or another, but we kept on looking.

I have always believed that things always happen for a reason, and I think the reason why Kinky and I never could find the perfect ranch was due to pure, simple fate. If it's not meant to be—it ain't gonna happen.

On Saturday, November 24, 2001, Kinky called me in the afternoon to tell me two exciting things, number one being that First Lady Laura Bush had agreed to do a luncheon for us in the spring, and number two being Kinky's father, Dr. Tom Friedman, had just told Kinky that we no longer needed to look for land, because he had decided to let us move our rescue ranch over to Echo Hill! That was one of the best days I'd had for good news, and I shall never forget it.

A few weeks later, on a cold, foggy, rainy afternoon, Tony and I drove over to Echo Hill Ranch, because Tom wanted to have a meeting with Kinky, Tony, and me; we were to meet at the Friedman dump, on the northeast side of the ranch. When we arrived, Tom and his wife, Edythe, Kinky, Marcie, Copper Love, and Ray Pump were waiting for us. Tom took me aside, and we walked over to the dump, which was a giant hole in the ground used for trash burning. As we stood there in the cold rain, Tom told me that he thought this location would be the perfect place for us to have the rescue ranch. He then pointed to the west and told me the view was absolutely beautiful, even though on that day the fog had covered it, and there was no view—just fog. He and I then shook hands.

When we returned to everyone, Tom asked us to get into the car for a brief talk. We all climbed into the Cadillac, and discussed the details concerning the move, and the meeting was then promptly ended. We had a deal! It was official: the rescue ranch was leaving Utopia and moving to Paradise—and the most beautiful ranch in the Texas Hill Country.

In December, Tony hit the ground running. Our good friends and volunteers Bethany Clark, her dad, Ralph Clark, Nick Marsh, Max Swafford, Keith Keese, and Linden Dokken went to work cutting brush, trimming trees, and digging post holes, on the weekends. While Tony and Maribeth put up fence during the week, Ray Pump and his son, Chris, built a well house, filled in the dump, strung electrical wiring, and worked on the plumbing, among many other things. I helped some with the work but mostly stayed at the rescue ranch in Utopia to conduct business, as well as arranging for a septic tank, phone service, etc.

This was all very costly, but thanks to our volunteers, Kinky's always-open checkbook, and the generosity of Jeff and Mary Erramouspe—the impossible was done! The new rescue ranch became more beautiful with every day that passed. And the view that Tom had told me about was absolutely to die for.

When friends of the Friedman family would call to ask where our new rescue ranch was located on Echo Hill, I would always jokingly say, "You know where the dump is? Well, that's where we are—and it's paradise!"

During the building of our new rescue ranch, our friends Jana Jackson and her daughter, Jenna, Lindy Padgett, and Kim Prest helped us move our two donkeys, Roy and Gabby, over to Echo Hill. Roy and Gabby are brothers, born under the sign of Libra, and are the two sweetest, biggest beggars that you've ever met. When they arrived at Echo Hill Ranch, Kinky fell in love with them and vice-versa. In fact, everyone who comes to the rescue ranch falls in love with them at first sight and wants to adopt them. But they are not up for adoption, because we love them so much and have made them ranch mascots.

Every morning since Roy and Gabby's arrival at the ranch, they magically show up at Kinky's back porch, if he is at the ranch, to beg for apples. Kinky, being the animal lover that he is, can't resist them and dutifully feeds them apples every day. And, one time, when Kinky was out of apples, he fed them donuts—which they loved even more than the apples.

Meanwhile, back at the ranch, progress marched on until it was all finally done. It was now time to move our dogs to their new digs!

Paradise, here we come. With the help of our volunteers Jim and Liz Cravotta, Vicki and Harry Gartrell, and Jenna and Jana Jackson, we were able to move all fifty dogs in just two trips to Echo Hill Ranch.

During the loading of the dogs, there was only one mishap—and that was me. I had my hand wrapped around Spot's collar, and was fixin' to attach a leash to him, when he jumped up and twisted in the air, again and again, causing his collar to tighten around my middle finger. Before Tony could cut the dog collar off with his pocketknife, my middle finger was bleeding and broken and had turned as black as an olive. Since that put me out of commission, Maribeth came to the rescue and took over my job of loading the dogs and transporting our precious cargo over to Echo Hill.

As soon as they were gone, I went inside to soak my finger.

On the Road Again

Wednesday afternoon, February 20, 2002, only one hour after we had successfully moved all of the dogs over to Echo Hill Ranch, I learned that my eighty-foot-long trailer was too long to make the move over there. Kinky was in Sydney, Australia, winding up a tour, so I called Kinky's dad, Dr. Tom Friedman, for advice. He and I put our heads together and decided that we should cut my twenty-year-old, beautiful trailer (that I love) in half—but were we wrong.

The bottom line was that if we did, my trailer would catch on fire and burn down to the wheels, because it would take a welding torch to cut the trailer in half. Suddenly, it had become quite evident to Tony and me that we were fixin' to become homeless (trailerless) people in a matter of a few days, once we moved over to the new rescue ranch at Echo Hill. Knowing that I was depressed, my nerves were frayed, and now I had to deal with my middle finger being broken, our good friend Nick Marsh, from Utopia, volunteered to camp out with the dogs at Echo Hill for that night.

On Thursday morning, Kinky called from Australia and talked me into spending the night at his Lodge that night while Tony stayed in Utopia. Everything went fine until some wild coyotes started howling, scaring me half to death. The following afternoon, after returning to Utopia, Tony and I packed the vehicles and headed back to Echo Hill Ranch with our thirteen dogs and two howling cats to spend the night together and keep watch over the rescued animals. That was fun.

When we arrived at Echo Hill, Tony and I fed the dogs and then cleaned their pens. Then we drove over to spend the night in the Friedman's "White Trailer" across the creek. As we happily unpacked our bags and unloaded our animals, the one thing that we didn't need to happen happened: a blue norther blew in, and it was suddenly colder than cold. Wanting to remain happy campers, we blew it off, sorta.

With our thirteen dogs and two cats all inside the trailer, our next surprise came when the ancient space heater in the White Trailer decided to die the minute that we turned it on. By now, the temperature inside the trailer was only ten degrees warmer than it was outside.

By eight o'clock, the inside temperature had dropped to thirty-two degrees, and our cats, Minnie Pearl and Lucky, were screaming mad, racing from one end of the trailer to the other and knocking down our little dogs who were innocently standing in their path. The dogs soon appeared depressed and began acting like they were being punished; I started crying because I wasn't sure about leaving Utopia, nor was I happy about being so cold, and I was worried about our pets being so upset, etc. But, God bless Tony, because while all of this was going on inside the trailer, he had disappeared to the bedroom and began stacking blanket after blanket onto the double bed mattress lying on the floor in the hopes that we might not freeze to death that night.

Fifteen minutes after Tony had the bed made, as the winds howled outside, he and I climbed down into the bed before turning off the lamp.

Within seconds, all thirteen of our dogs jumped on the bed to keep warm, but they kept sliding off because there was so little room. The cats, who were now madder than two wet hens, howled, emitting noises that we had never heard before. Minnie and Lucky sounded like they were being tortured, but, fortunately, the hard blowing wind outside muffled their cries.

Around ten o'clock that night, we were all still wide awake, because our dogs couldn't decide where to sleep. By midnight, all thirteen dogs were asleep in our bed—they had decided to sleep on top of us. I woke up around one-thirty, because I couldn't move my legs; they had no feeling in them because Abbie, our six-month-old wannabe black Lab, was sleeping on top of them. I quietly got her moved while Tony and Yoda took turns snoring. As luck would have it, as soon as I had removed Abbie from my lower body, Yoda began farting under the covers.

Somehow, I finally fell asleep for at least thirty minutes before being rudely awakened again. It was not Jack Frost nipping at my toes but Toto biting my nose—he was mad. Toto, our little Terrier (terrorist) mix, aka "the dictator," had a rule when it came to sleeping arrangements. His rule was simple: no one was allowed to move once they were in bed. If you moved, he would bite you.

It was my fault, of course, since I had moved, and therefore I deserved my punishment. I should have known better since I have been bitten countless times by Toto for moving violations, but I guess I forgot. Fortunately for me, it was not a bad bite, and I had very little loss of blood. Once again, I fell back to sleep, even though my nose was throbbing.

The straw that broke the camel's back happened when our ticked-off three-legged cat, Lucky, intentionally dragged his front claw across my forehead, causing me much pain and more blood loss. Scared to move because Toto might bite me again, I just laid there and counted the number of blankets on our bed until I drifted off to Neverland. My last count was seven.

At five a.m., I got out of bed and whispered, "I'm leaving. I don't know if I should go to the Kerrville emergency room or back home to Utopia."

Tony looked at me with shock. "What happened to your face?" he asked.

"I moved," I said, "Toto bit my nose, and Lucky decided to get even and played tic-tac-toe on my forehead."

With that said, Tony and I packed quickly, loaded up our animals, and left the White Trailer within twenty minutes. Before leaving, Tony cleaned the dog pens, while I quickly fed the dogs, as all the while the two angry cats screamed nonstop inside the vehicle. With the chores done, we drove the forty-two miles back to Utopia with our thirteen dogs and two angry cats.

By the time we arrived in Utopia, the sun was shining, and the temperature had already reached the low forties and was climbing. After we unloaded the animals and turned on the heat in the trailer, I braced myself and looked into the mirror.

What I saw was very frightening. First off, I realized that overnight I had turned into an albino—my hair was solid white, and my eyebrows looked like fallen flakes of snow resting on dirt. The only thing red on my face, besides my bloodshot eyes, was the blood on the tip of my nose, compliments of Toto. And my forehead looked like a treasure map drawn with a red pencil, with an "X" marking the spot right above my right brown-and-white eyebrow. To top it all off, my broken middle finger was throbbing.

Once again, as I stared into the mirror, I began to cry. Even though Tony did not want to join my self-pity party, he helped doctor my wounds. By the time he had finished, I had one of those little round Band-Aids on the tip of my nose and a large patch covering my forehead. Trying to cheer me up, Tony put my prized Imus cap on my head and promised me that I looked fine. Knowing that he was lying to me, I jokingly held up my hand with my broken middle finger and saluted him.

Later that afternoon, Kinky called from the airport in Australia to check on us. By the time I had told him about our little overnight adventure, he had me laughing at the whole situation. Before hanging up, he reminded me that he would be back at Echo Hill Ranch Sunday afternoon, and he would then take over the job of babysitting the rescue dogs until we got ourselves moved over there. That was a relief to me, and I looked forward to seeing him again.

With that conversation ended, I reached out and started another one. I called our talented friend Sage Ferrero, who, at the time, was running Kinky's award-winning website (thanks to her) and asked her if she wanted to spend the night over at Echo Hill Ranch that night. Not knowing what all we had been through the night before, she gladly accepted my invitation to babysit the rescue ranch that night. As Sage babysat the dogs over at Echo Hill that night, Tony and I slept peaceably with thirteen dogs and two worn-out cats in Utopia.

Sunday evening, Kinky called to let us know that he was back at Echo Hill and that the dogs were doing fine. Things quickly got better from that point on. Every morning, Tony would go over to Echo Hill to feed the dogs and to clean their pens. Then he would stay over there for several more hours before returning home. Kinky seemed to enjoy his job of babysitting the dogs and every afternoon would show up with hot dogs or treats to give to the incredible dogs that called our rescue ranch home.

On Monday, February 25th, Ray Pump came over to haul my writing cabin over to Echo Hill Ranch. We quickly realized that we needed forklifts to lift my cabin onto Ray's trailer. Tony called our good friends Sid, Sid, Jr., and Tommy Mauldin, owners of Utopia Builders Supply, to ask if we could borrow their forklifts; of course, their answer was yes. Within fifteen minutes, Sid, Jr., and Tommy showed up at the ranch with their forklifts and lifted my building onto Ray's trailer. Then Ray, his son, Chris, Tony, Maribeth, and I took off to deliver my cabin to Echo Hill Ranch. When we arrived at Echo Hill, our friend and neighbor Robert Selement was already there waiting for us with his backhoe. Thirty minutes later, my little 12' × 12' cabin was off of Ray's trailer and planted on Echo Hill soil! The following day, Ray hooked up the electricity.

During the next few days, Kinky and I were back and forth on the phone concerning moving our trailer—if it could be moved at all because of the narrow turns and switchbacks. Kinky called his good friends Allan and Gloria King about the trouble that we might have moving the trailer through their beautiful ranch, Deer Valley, and their response to Kinky was to do whatever was necessary to their ranch to get our trailer moved to Echo Hill. Thank goodness for good neighbors!

The only problem left was trying to find someone that could move our trailer. It seemed everyone in the trailer moving business was way overbooked, and their earliest time estimates were two to three months. At one point, Kinky called to tell me that he was going to call his buddy U.S. Congressman Lamar Smith, to ask if he could help us get the trailer moved. Fortunately, he didn't have to resort to that.

Thankfully, on Thursday afternoon, Tony found a man who said he would move it. Then Tony and the man drove over to Echo Hill to make sure that he could get our eighty-foot-long trailer through the narrow bridge that was surrounded by hundred-year-old cypress trees on Deer Valley Ranch—and his answer was yes.

There is only one good thing to say about trailers: moving the contents is easy. The only packing that Tony and I had to do was to take everything out of the cabinets and off the walls, and pack them into boxes. In the course of two evenings, our trailer was ready to be moved!

Before six-thirty on Sunday morning, March 3, 2002, after taping the refrigerator closed with duct tape, we made a secret pact. We decided that Lucky and Minnie Pearl, our two cats, should ride inside the trailer, locked in our bedroom closet, so they wouldn't freak out again. I also had to promise Tony that I would take the heat if anything bad happened to our cats while on the move. And we both agreed not to tell Kinky about "Operation Catnap," because we knew he would worry himself sick about them.

With that decided, Tony and I drove our thirteen dogs over to Echo Hill Ranch and put them in the newly erected, unoccupied pig pen. After feeding all of the rescue ranch dogs and cleaning their pens, we drove back over to Utopia—dogless.

At ten o'clock sharp, the trailer mover showed up to move our trailer. Knowing that it would take a few hours to prepare our trailer for the move, I went ahead and left, because I was sad about leaving my little ranch that I loved so much and did not want to watch my trailer being pulled away.

When I arrived at Echo Hill Ranch, Kinky and I passed the hours nervously drinking coffee in his kitchen, as he tried to cheer me up about moving to his ranch. Even though I was pretty depressed about leaving Utopia and all of my dear friends, I knew that I would soon be fine and grow to love Echo Hill Ranch as much as I had loved mine.

Around five o'clock that evening, the trailer had not yet arrived, but a blue norther did! I left Kinky's Lodge and went over to my small cabin to turn the heater on and be with my dogs. My thirteen dogs kept me company inside my cozy cabin as I waited for my trailer.

By eight o'clock that night, the temperature had plummeted to twenty-nine degrees and was still falling—but still no trailer. I was beginning to get very concerned about Tony and the trailer and was wondering why they weren't there yet. Then my dogs started barking. I got out of my chair and saw the headlights of Kinky's car approaching. Even though it was now down to eighteen degrees outside, Kinky had good news and bad news to tell me.

My trailer had arrived! It was only two miles away, but it was stuck at Deer Valley Ranch, at the first creek crossing, and was blocking the road so that nobody could get in or out. And the only way to get my home to me was for Robert Selement and Ray Pump to bulldoze a ledge on Deer Valley Ranch! Kinky told me that they were already in the process of moving the land, and the trailer hopefully should arrive in a couple of hours.

Kinky stayed and talked with me for about an hour and then left to go back to his Lodge; fortunately for me, he did not notice our cats were missing.

At precisely 1:14 in the wee hours, Tony drove up to the cabin to tell me our trailer had made it through Deer Valley Ranch and would be arriving in a matter of minutes, and the cats were doing fine! Next came our trailer; it had to be backed into the rescue ranch so our front door faced the beautiful view to the west. After our mobile home was parked, the exhausted trailer mover asked Tony if it would be all right with him if he came back when the sun was up to tie down the trailer and set it up. Tony told him it was fine, and the trailer mover left the ranch.

Before going to bed, Tony took the flashlight and went to the trailer to check on our cats. When he returned to my little cabin he told me the cats were doing great, as if nothing had happened or changed. That night, Tony and I made a bed of cushions from the couch and chairs with our thirteen dogs snuggling close.

The next morning, Kinky came over and invited us over for coffee and breakfast. After we had discussed the trailer move, I told Kinky about the cats riding over to Echo Hill Ranch in the closet. He loved it, and then congratulated us on having come up with such a brilliant plan. Within the next two weeks, our phones were connected, and our pigs were delivered to us by Lindy and Kim Prest—we were back to rescuing animals!

PART SIX

Life with the Kinkster

Alfred Hitchcock

Our "watch dog," Blue

Chef Daniel—
Thanksgiving '05

Ben & Tony

Adoption conference with
the Kinkster

Yoda

Porky Pig

F-150

Kinky vs. Cousin Nancy

The ongoing battle between Kinky and me began on Monday, May 17, 1999.

On that morning, Tony and I rescued four dogs from the Kerrville Pound. One of the dogs that we rescued was a small, approximately two-year-old, cream-colored Poodle/Terrier cross I named Toto, because he looked like the little dog in *The Wizard of Oz*.

When we first saw Toto in his pen, he was barking at the top of his lungs trying to get our attention. He was standing up on his hind legs, furiously clawing at the gate for us to come rescue him and get him out of there. He didn't want to die!

After our many trips to the pound, Tony and I discovered that some of the dogs know they are going to be killed, while other dogs, especially the puppies, don't seem to have a clue as they romp and play. Toto knew!

After leaving the pound, Tony and I took the four dogs to Hoegemeyer Animal Clinic and dropped them off for their checkups, worming, shots, and spaying or neutering. Two days later, I went to Kerrville to pick up our four new rescues; they were ready to come to the rescue ranch. Kinky had asked me to stop by Echo Hill on my way back to Utopia, so he could meet our new dogs. So, I did.

The minute Kinky laid eyes on Toto he fell in love with him. After a quick cup of Kona coffee with Kinky, I drove the dogs to the rescue ranch. Since Toto was so small, and might get picked on by bigger dogs, Tony and I decided to let Toto live in our trailer until he was adopted.

That evening, Kinky called to tell us that he had found a great home for Toto. Tony and I were glad to hear the news but didn't find it terribly surprising, since Kinky had found good homes for nearly half of our rescued dogs. After Kinky made several phone calls on Toto's behalf, his friend Dennis Laviage, from Houston, wanted Toto for his aging parents. He told Kinky that his parents had recently lost their little dog from old age, and, when Dennis told them about Toto, they were excited and couldn't wait to get him. Dennis guaranteed Kinky that Toto would live in the lap of luxury and be spoiled rotten.

On May 22, 1999, I drove Toto over to Kinky's, so Dennis could pick him up and take him back to Houston. On the entire forty-two-mile trip over to Kinky's, Toto sat in my lap. When we arrived at Kinky's ranch, Toto would not leave my side. Kinky informed me that Dennis had gone swimming and suggested that we hike over to the swimming hole to show him Toto. I didn't have any other plans that Saturday afternoon, so the three of us took off to go find Dennis.

It had been a while since the south fork had been mowed and poor Toto was having a hard time keeping up with us. It seemed for every ten steps that we took, Toto would catch a sticker in his foot and need to have it removed. At this rate, I figured it would be dark before we made it to the swimming hole, which was only about a half mile away from us. So Kinky picked Toto up and carried him the rest of the distance.

Dennis was delighted to meet Toto, but the feeling wasn't mutual. As Dennis dried himself off, Toto pawed at my legs to be picked up and held, so I picked him up and held him for a while. Every time that I put Toto's feet back on the ground he pawed until I picked him up again. When it was time to return to Kinky's Lodge, Toto went the distance in Kinky's arms.

When I started to leave Echo Hill to go back home, Toto jumped out of Dennis's arms, ran to me, and jumped into my truck. That's when I knew Toto really loved me and didn't want to go to Houston—he wanted to go home with me. I gave Toto a kiss, handed him back to Kinky, and then drove off feeling somewhat sad about Toto.

By the time I arrived back at the ranch I had the issue about Toto settled. I knew that Toto would miss me for a while, but after a few days of receiving constant attention he would forget me and live out the rest of his life happily.

Oh, boy—was I ever wrong, again! In less than forty-eight hours Dennis had called Kinky and would be returning one unhappy little dog to him immediately. The reason being that Toto was miserable and would not have anything to do with his parents, and when they would try to pet him he would bite them and then run under their couch to hide. Toto was obviously homesick.

Kinky called to tell us the news about Toto, and, before we could get a word in edgewise, he told us that he was glad Toto was coming back, because he had decided to adopt him. End of story—sort of.

Toto lived happily with Kinky for about a week. On the seventh day, Kinky's big, sweet dog, Mr. Magoo, tried to murder Toto!

Kinky called me after returning from an emergency visit to the Hoegemeyer Animal Clinic. He told me that he had taken Mr. Magoo and Toto down to the swimming hole for a swim. Everything was going well until he threw a tennis ball for Mr. Magoo to catch, and Toto tried to get it, too. Mr. Magoo reacted by biting Toto on the top of his head, causing him to bleed profusely. Kinky then hollered at Mr. Magoo to stop it and then dove into the water to rescue Toto from drowning. He then rushed Toto to see Dr. Hoegemeyer. After a thorough checkup, a shot, and some bandaging, Toto returned with Kinky to Echo Hill Ranch. Dr. Hoegemeyer had assured Kinky that Toto would be as good as new in a short period of time.

Kinky told me that he was furious with Mr. Magoo about his jealousy and asked me if I would come over in the morning to pick up Toto and take him back to my place. Kinky was sad but certain that Mr. Magoo and Toto had become mortal enemies over the attack and felt that Toto would be much happier and safer in Tony's and my trailer.

I agreed with him and picked Toto up the following morning. Much to Kinky's disappointment, Toto couldn't wait to leave Echo Hill Ranch and Mr. Magoo.

When I pulled up to the Lodge, Toto came running and jumped into my pickup before I could get out of it. He showered me with kisses and stayed by my side as Kinky and I visited. I could tell that Kinky was sad to give up Toto, but he was doing it for unselfish reasons; Toto needed to be safe.

After Toto came to live with Tony and me, we discovered quickly that he had two personalities, like Dr. Jekyll or Mr. Hyde. He wasn't a schizophrenic or bipolar—he was just half poodle and half terrier. When in poodle mode he was a sweet, affectionate little fella. When he was in his terrier mode he became a terrorist to be reckoned with—he had no fear.

Every time that Kinky would come to the rescue ranch, Toto would get excited and shower him with kisses and want to be held. Kinky would often tease me that Toto was his son and that Toto loved him more than he loved me. I would jokingly argue that Toto loved me more, was extremely possessive of me, and had never wanted to live with Kinky in the first place. Kinky would fire back that if not for Mr. Magoo wanting to kill him, Toto would be much happier at his ranch in Medina.

Kinky and I had a showdown at high noon, in my backyard, on March 25, 2000, in front of Don Imus's MSNBC crew. It was the day that our Dwight Yoakam concert was to be held that night in Helotes, Texas, at the Floore Country Store. Imus had sent down his crew to capture the event in order to help promote our rescue ranch.

After Kinky had given the MSNBC crew an interview, he challenged me, in front of the cameras, to do a "tug of love" with Toto. Kinky wanted to prove to the world, once and for all, that Toto loved him more than he loved me. I accepted the challenge and bet Kinky one dollar that I would win. Everyone marched to my backyard, and then Kinky and I went into the yard with Toto.

Kinky and I took opposite ends of the yard, and, on the count of three, without using dog treats, we called Toto to come to us. In a matter of seconds I had won, of course! Toto had run immediately to me and jumped into my arms. As I held Toto proudly in my arms, Kinky conceded to the world that today, Toto did love me more, but he knew in his heart it had not been a "toto loss" for him. He had not given up and challenged me again, the next time he came over, to prove Toto's love.

To date, Toto still lives with us and definitely loves me more. He proves it every night when Tony and I go to bed. As soon as we are in bed, he hops up and lies down, next to my head, on my pillow. During the night if Tony or I move, he lets out a sharp bark and then growls for a few seconds.

I can also prove that Toto loves me more because of his possessiveness of me. In the evenings, when Tony and I are watching television together, he sits in my lap and growls at any dog that passes by my chair to let them know that I am his and he is mine—until death do us part!

The Rooster Crows at Noon

In the fall of 2000, our good friend Bethany Clark called the rescue ranch and asked for help. She had an emergency!

Bethany had a pet rooster named Chuggie, and the two of them were inseparable, or so Chuggie thought.

Bethany and Chuggie had been together for years, and, like most males, was territorial. Any time that Bethany had company, Chuggie would not let them get out of their vehicles, and if someone was dumb enough to get out of their truck—Chuggie would beat them up.

Chuggie was a proud, big, red and yellow rooster who patrolled Bethany's ranch from sunup till dinnertime. At dinnertime, he would be invited into Bethany's trailer to spend the night in a basket in Bethany's kitchen. Chuggie hated dinner guests, too, because he would have to wait outside until the guests had left. Maybe that explains why he would chase them to their cars as they were leaving to go home.

Chuggie proved himself to be a fine, fit rooster, because Chuggie, Jr., was born. Chuggie, Jr., looked just like his father, and every time that Bethany called for Chuggie, Sr., Junior would come running too, causing a fight to erupt between the father and son.

Tired of the constant confrontations, Bethany chose to rename Chug, Jr., Jesse, but the name change did no good—the two of them still continued to fight. Chuggie, Sr., was jealous of his handsome young son and felt threatened, so Bethany took matters into her own hands: she dialed the rescue ranch and asked us if we could take Jesse.

Being that she was a dear friend, our answer was yes.

The following day, Bethany drove over to the rescue ranch and hand-delivered Jesse to us. Tony immediately put him in with our chickens and it worked out. With all of our eyes glued to the pig and chicken pen, we watched Jesse, as soon as he was let down, strut proudly around the chickens as if showing off for them. Our chickens seemed oblivious to him, but Jesse didn't seem to care—he was in chicken heaven!

As soon as Bethany left the rescue ranch, I immediately renamed Jesse Alfred Hitchcock. My thinking is: new life, new name, and Alfred didn't seem to care; he was too busy making love.

The next morning, Tony and I got up really early so we could hear Alfred crow, but he didn't. We were disappointed, to say the least. Tony joked that maybe Alfred was too busy to crow because of all of his new-found girlfriends. The way Alfred was going after it, it actually did sorta make sense, but I was still disappointed.

My disappointment was soon erased when Alfred began crowing at straight up noon! He must have crowed for over ten minutes, and it was fantastic. Later that evening, Tony joked that he guessed Alfred Hitchcock was waiting until he had something to crow about; I believed it, because in no time flat, we had many little chicks running around the pen with their henpecking mothers following close behind them.

To this day, Alfred Hitchcock has never crowed in the morning or anytime else except noon. None of us has ever been able to figure it out, but it is fine. Alfred is as precise as Big Ben.

This past spring, Kinky brought out a group of reporters to see the rescue ranch and to meet the animals. His final destination was the pig pen, which is the closest pen to our house (trailer). The reporters were from some big news group, and they fell instantly in love with our pigs, Arnold, Porky, Babe, Lucy, Little Ricky Ricardo, Alice, and Laverne and Shirley. They took pictures of Butterball, the big white turkey, who thankfully has now survived three Thanksgivings, and the chickens that lay brown, blue, and green eggs.

After everyone was done meeting the animals, one of the reporters turned on a tape recorder and asked Kinky a question concerning his campaign for governor. The cameras began flashing, and, just as Kinky started to talk, Alfred Hitchcock did his thing—he crowed! Everyone laughed, and then waited for Kinky to speak. Once again, as Kinky began to speak, Alfred crowed. When the laughter subsided, after about one sentence had come out of Kinky's mouth, yes, Alfred crowed again.

Kinky puffed on his cigar and then explained to the reporters, "Alfred only crows at the crack of noon. What time is it?"

Tony answered, "One o'clock."

Kinky seized the moment and said, "He's not adjusted to the time change yet."

Stranger in the Night

Living within a half of a mile of the Kinkster has been quite exciting, and a lot of fun, to say the least. Since Tony and I moved ourselves and the rescue ranch to Echo Hill Ranch, back in March 2002, a number of strange and mysterious events have occurred.

One in particular happened back in the spring of 2002, nearly causing Kinky to have a heart attack and him and me to die. It was truly spooky.

Around 4:30 in the morning, with our rescue dogs outside howling at a beautiful, gigantic full moon, Tony and I were restless and unable to fall asleep. Unbeknownst to us at the time, Kinky too was having the very same problem over at his Lodge. When Kinky was just about to fall asleep, his five dogs started barking and then raced through the Lodge, escaping to the outside via their doggie door. The Friedmans then began barking wildly, as if they were trying to tell Kinky that something or someone was outside!

Frustrated, yet concerned, Kinky decided to get up and do the right thing: get his dogs back inside the Lodge. Only half awake, Kinky went to his kitchen and flipped on the lights—and then he nearly flipped out at what he saw before screaming "HELP!" at the top of his lungs! Unfortunately, neither Tony nor I heard Kinky's plea, because we had our own little rodeo going on outside trying to chase some twenty wild hogs off of the rescue ranch.

Kinky stood frozen in his footsteps, in his kitchen, as he stared back into the eyes that had terrified him! Standing about three-and-a-half to four feet tall, outside the glass kitchen door, was this little old man staring at Kinky with intense eyes that never blinked once.

Step by step, Kinky cautiously inched his way to the door. The little man never budged an inch but continued to stare at Kinky without changing his serious expression. Kinky then stepped back and moved over by the refrigerator to find that the little man had moved too. He was now staring directly at Kinky from the kitchen window. Kinky jumped to the side and the little man jumped sideways, too! Then Kinky left the kitchen to find his glasses and gun.

When Kinky returned, armed and dangerous, the little man was still patiently waiting for him outside. When Kinky put on his eyeglasses, he burst into laughter—he recognized the face. It was his good friend Willie Nelson!

Well, it wasn't really Willie in the flesh, but it was Willie's face on the front of the black T-shirt that Kinky was wearing. Quickly, Kinky put two and two together, realizing that what he had seen outside was the reflection of his T-shirt in the glass door and windows.

Thank goodness Kinky didn't have a heart attack that night. My near-death experience was caused by Kinky telling his story to us, the following morning, while I was eating a breakfast taco. When Kinky showed us the Willie Nelson T-shirt that had caused all of the trouble, I laughed so hard, I nearly choked to death.

Battle of the Spoons

For the past several years, Kinky has paid for the dogs at the rescue ranch to be served hot home- (trailer-) cooked Thanksgiving and Christmas dinners. The chefs for these holiday dinners have been Ben Welch, Will Wallace, Daniel Hudson, Nancy Doyle, from the City of Hope in Chicago, Kinky, Tony, and myself. We have a blast doing it, and every single one of our dogs at the rescue ranch loves their hot, delicious meals and they go crazy when we serve them their holiday dinners. The dogs become so excited about their dinners, they act like they have never eaten food before.

We do the cooking inside our trailer, which generally takes up to two hours to prepare. If Kinky does the cooking, it is more fun, but it takes three hours or more.

Our standard recipe that we cook up takes three ten-pound sacks of mixed vegetables (lima beans, peas, corn, green beans, and carrots). Next we add three large jars of olive oil, two pounds of shredded cheddar cheese, six cans of spinach, four large jars of minced garlic, seven dozen eggs, ten pounds of ground hamburger meat, ten pounds of ground turkey meat, and a few bags of broccoli, squash, and cauliflower. Then we cook it all up in the oven until it is hot.

The last thing we do after pulling the food out of the oven is to add dry dog food to the mixture. That is the guys' job, and they have perfected their procedure of mixing in the dry dog food to a fine art. Without spilling a morsel, they use four large plastic buckets and divide the heated food equally into the buckets. Next, they use two giant drills, equipped with long paddles, to mix in the final ingredient, the dry dog food. After the food has been properly mixed, it is time to go outside and serve the dogs their dinners using large wooden kitchen spoons.

We use the huge wooden spoons, because at least one spoon ends up broken off at its end by some overly anxious dog waiting to be served his or her holiday dinner. When a spoon gets the end bitten off of it, I write on the spoon with a marker the date, the name of the person who was using it for feeding, and the name of the dog responsible. Since we have been doing this for years, I am hoping that by the next holiday season I'll have enough spoons collected for Tony to make me a wind chime for the front porch.

Thanksgiving 2004, Ben, Tony, and I prepared the dinner. Right before we were ready to go outside, Kinky called wanting to know if he could come over and help us serve the dogs. My answer, of course, was yes, and to hurry up! When I told everyone that Kinky was coming over, Tony remarked, "Thank God and Greyhounds he didn't offer to help us cook it. Shoot, we would have been cooking until midnight if that had happened."

Ben, Tony, and I were already outside by the pens when Kinky arrived. Before starting to serve the dinner, Kinky made a bet with us that the dogs would not eat their vegetables. We knew better, so we made the bet with him, knowing full well that we would win.

Before the banquet began, while Tony tuned in a football game to be broadcast over our PA system for the dogs to enjoy, Ben and I flipped a coin. I won the coin toss, which meant that Kinky and I would feed the dogs on the east side of the ranch, and Ben and Tony would feed the dogs on the west side.

When we embarked on feeding the fifty or more dogs, they began howling with excitement because they couldn't wait until it was their turn to be served their hot holiday dinner. After Kinky and I had fed about half of the dogs on our side, Kinky hollered at me. When I looked over, Kinky was smiling and holding up his broken spoon that Rufus had just bitten the end off of.

Knowing that we would lose a spoon or two in the feeding frenzy, I always carried spares with me. I tossed Kinky another one, and he and I finished feeding our side before Tony and Ben did theirs. While waiting for Ben and Tony to finish, Kinky told me that he could not get over the dogs breaking the ends off of the spoons, and that he was amazed at how fast the dogs had consumed their dinners—like it was their last supper.

When Tony and Ben finished feeding their side, we decided that the four of us would go from pen to pen to see if all of the dogs had eaten their vegetables. It ended up that we lost the bet with Kinky because of one dog—Molly Ivins. She had licked her dish sparkling clean except for the peas, which she had neatly stacked into a small pile beside her dish!

Being the poor sports that we were, Tony, Ben, and I teased Kinky that he would never see the money we owed him from the bet. Kinky didn't seem to care at all. He told us that being a part of the dog's Thanksgiving feast had made his day, and, for the very first time in his life, he couldn't wait for Christmas to come!

Viva Las Vacation!

Operating a rescue ranch is extremely time consuming; basically, you are married to it twenty-four/seven. Fortunately, Tony and I are homebodies, and, as Kinky likes to put it, we "don't get out much."

It is hard for Tony and me to even go to lunch, a party, or visit our friends together, because we don't like leaving the animals unattended for even two or three hours. A couple of times a week, Tony and I do go to Kerrville or Bandera to eat lunch, leaving Maribeth Couch, Ben Welch, or Will Wallace in charge, and we are fine with that. Otherwise, it is not a problem for us to stay put. Fortunately, our friends are understanding about our situation, so they come to the rescue ranch to visit us rather than having Tony and me leave the ranch to go visit them.

Because Tony and I are in our fifties, we also have night vision problems. We basically never go out at night, because headlights blind us, and that is dangerous in the Texas Hill Country because of the roaming deer and wandering wild hogs that cause car wrecks, killing several people every year. And besides, we enjoy being home with our animals and going to bed early. We would rather do that than be a statistic or a headline in one of the local newspapers.

That we don't get out much drives Kinky totally crazy! He is forever telling us to take a break and leave the ranch, so we won't get burned out. Because Kinky has selective hearing, he doesn't understand that we love it here, and leaving the ranch would drive Tony and me crazy with worry. For seven years, this has been an ongoing battle among the three of us, and Kinky finally won it Memorial Day Weekend 2005.

In early April 2005, while we were all eating breakfast together, Kinky persuaded Tony and me to go with him to Las Vegas for a few days. He made us an offer that we couldn't refuse. He told us that he would get everything comped for us, and our only costs would be our airline tickets and gambling money.

Two days later, after making arrangements with Ben to babysit the rescue ranch, the three of us purchased our airline tickets, and the countdown to our Las Vegas trip began. Kinky called his friends to invite them to join us, but, unfortunately, Kent Perkins and his wife, Ruth Buzzi, couldn't join us, because they were going to be spending Memorial Day Weekend at the Indy 500 with James Garner; fortunately, Mike McGovern agreed to meet us out there. We were set and ready to go— we thought.

"Hello, Houston? We've got a problem." Tony got cold feet and decided he wasn't going to Las Vegas, just ten days before our planned liftoff. Our countdown was now postponed. When I told Kinky about Tony not wanting to go to Las Vegas, because he didn't want to leave the dogs and also hated flying, Kinky was disappointed and told me that we needed to work on Tony. We made a secret plan and it worked.

After hours of my begging Tony, and Kinky explaining to him over and over again how safe air travel was, Tony caved in and did what any good astronaut would do—he said yes, because my talking had worn him out. After our countdown was resumed, the three of us plotted how we were going to hook up at the San Antonio airport.

We decided to meet at 6:00 p.m. in front of the Southwest Airlines ticket counter, two hours before blast off. Kinky would be coming in from Hunt, Texas—following a "meet and greet" for his bid for governor—and Tony and I would be driving in from the rescue ranch, some seventy miles away. We then synchronized our watches.

Kinky was the first to arrive at the airport and panicked somewhat when he couldn't find us; that was because we weren't there yet. Ten minutes later, upon our arrival, we couldn't find Kinky, because he was surrounded by about thirty fans, talking politics and signing autographs. Tony called Kinky on his cell phone to find out where he was. Kinky told him to turn around and look over at the baggage area, and then he waved his cowboy hat at Tony.

After Kinky signed his last autograph, we went through security— and we passed! Having over an hour to kill, Kinky decided that we all needed to drink a beer to help relax Tony. As soon as we sat down on the barstools, the bartender asked Kinky for an autograph, as did every drunk in there. It ended up taking two beers for Tony to relax. After wetting our whistles, we left four empty beer mugs on the bar and proceeded to the boarding area near the launch site.

Thank God and Greyhounds our flight was fast and smooth. The three of us passed away the time by watching the many slideshows that I had made of our rescue ranch dogs on my computer. Kinky's favorite slideshow was the one I did on the Echo Hill Camp kids daily walking our dogs and taking them swimming.

Tony was most definitely the happiest person on the plane when we made a successful landing in Las Vegas. Our taxicab driver made me the happiest person on earth to ever get out of a cab, because of his reckless driving. I figured that he must have been from England, because he kept driving down the wrong side of the street. And Kinky was, for certain, the happiest man in Las Vegas when we arrived at the Flamingo Hotel—he was ready to gamble.

After we had disposed of our luggage in our adjacent rooms on the twenty-fourth floor, we went down to the casino area to find Mike McGovern, hook up with Kinky's friend, Kelly, and then enjoy a late dinner.

During our meal, Kelly pulled out some pictures of her family to show us. Kinky teased her that no one goes around carrying that many pictures of their family to show to people. To prove his point, he asked me if I had ever carried around pictures to show to people.

My answer was, "No, Kinky, I just carry around my slideshows."

Following dinner, Mike went to play some serious hands of poker, and the four of us went to the slot machines to make investments. It ended up that the talking, singing Elvis slot machines were the most fun. That night the Elvises kept all of us laughing while putting a lot of change back into our pockets, which seemed to have invisible holes in them.

Our last night in Las Vegas, Kinky treated Kelly, Tony, and me to the Penn & Teller Show at the renowned Rio Hotel. Unfortunately, Mike was in a poker tournament and unable to go with us. And not just because we probably had the best seats in the house, the Penn & Teller Show was an incredibly great time. Following their show, while Penn and Teller signed autographs, Penn's wife, who was expecting to go into labor that night with their first child, found Kinky and invited all of us backstage for drinks and a visit. We were all excited about going backstage, even though we were unaware at the time that we were fixin' to see the biggest show on earth!

All of us visited backstage for about an hour, and there were a lot of laughs; then came a knock on the door. A hotel security man answered the knock to find a young man and woman who had been invited ear-lier to come backstage to meet Penn and Teller. They came into the room and introduced themselves to everyone.

They started off by telling us that they were big fans of Penn and Teller and had driven from Montana just to see their show. Then they told us that they were dating each other, and she worked for him, doing an act that she had developed in his traveling circus. With everyone's curiosity piqued, Kinky or Penn asked them what her act was. Her boyfriend explained that she could lift all kinds of heavy things off of the ground using only her boobs, and the name of her act was Boobzilla!

Someone in the room asked how, and the next thing we knew, she pulled her shirt off, and, standing bare-breasted in front of us, told us that her bra size was a Double-L and that her boobs were still growing! It was definitely a Kodak Moment, but no one had a wide-angle lens. Her boyfriend bragged about her being able to lift heavy chairs, etc., while she slipped her T-shirt back on. Then she told us that she was going for the record of having the largest, untampered-with, natural boobs in the world!

Later, on the way back to our hotel, in the cab, we all agreed that she would most likely break the world record, because none of us had ever seen such large breasts.

The following morning, we left Las Vegas and returned home safely to the rescue ranch. And yes, we watched my slideshows again.

Recently, when Kinky, Tony, and I were discussing what to do next year, for our next vacation, Tony suggested that the three of us drive up to Montana to see the mountains.

Kinky shot back with, "Which mountains?" causing all of us to laugh.

Green, Green Grass of Home

As everyone knows, dogs have two different kinds of barks. One is the happy, playful bark, and the other is alarmingly serious—and dogs can tell the difference between them, too.

In the past seven years, when the rescued dogs start barking outside, Tony and I have come to rely on our seven house dogs to let us know if we need to go outside to check things out, or if we shouldn't worry about it, because it is probably just a visiting squirrel, armadillo, wild hog, porcupine, or deer causing all of the commotion. So, when our dogs pick up on the barking dogs outside, we know there is trouble and head for the door, pronto!

It was approximately four-thirty in the morning, in late spring 2004, when the rescue ranch dogs outside went into a barking frenzy, causing our dogs inside the trailer to wake us up. We knew something wasn't right outside, so we got dressed quickly. As soon as Tony was dressed, he and his faithful sidekick Blue Heeler dog, Blue, went outside to check things out. After making some coffee, I went out on the porch and watched the beams of Tony's spotlight bouncing off in one direction after another. It was pitch black outside, and watching the bouncing beams of light reminded me of my old stoned hippie days, back in Fort Worth.

After about twenty minutes, the dogs quit barking, and Tony and Blue returned to the trailer—my light show was over. Tony told me that he couldn't find a thing, and he had no idea what had caused all of the ruckus. But little did he know that he was fixin' to find out fast!

No sooner had we come back inside our trailer than the telephone rang. Somebody was fixin' to reach out and touch someone, and I didn't want to be the one, so Tony bravely took the call. After Tony had answered the phone, I checked our caller ID—it was Kinky! That shot my blood pressure up a notch or two. As Tony said nothing, I was thinking, why in the world would Kinky be calling us at five o'clock in the morning? He never called us after two a.m.; it's his telephone etiquette.

Finally, when Tony hung up the phone, he told me, as he grabbed his shotgun and some bullets and was going out the front door with Blue by his side, that he was headed over to Kinky's, and I needed to lock the doors. He told me, as I followed him to the gate, that a strange pickup, with no headlights, had driven past Kinky's Lodge about an hour ago—headed for the South Flat.

As Tony and Blue drove off, I went back inside the trailer, locked the doors, and impatiently waited for about fifteen minutes, until I heard a shotgun blast. That was it! Like an idiot, I reacted in completely the wrong way—I drove over to Kinky's Lodge.

When I arrived at the Lodge, Kinky and Tony were outside, standing by the truck and not looking very happy with themselves.

"What in the world is going on?" I asked, as I joined them. "I heard the shotgun."

"It was poachers," Kinky answered, shaking his head.

"We killed 'em," Tony half-whispered, before the two of them burst out laughing.

"What?" I asked in disbelief.

"We're just kidding," Tony said. "It wasn't poachers at all—it was Mr. Hubble, an old-timer from Medina, who came out early to mow the South Flat before it got too hot. He's in his seventies."

"How can he mow in the dark?" I asked.

"Headlights—his tractor has headlights," Kinky teased.

"Why did you fire the shotgun then?" I asked.

"Kinky and I made a bet to see how fast you'd get over here," Tony said.

"And I won," Kinky bragged.

By the dawn's early light, Mr. Hubble had finished mowing the South Flat and gone home.

June teaching manners

Tony & Rodney

Tony and Mama

PART SEVEN

Keepin' on the Sunny Side

Albert Einstein

Cousin Nancy & Mama

Kinky & Stella

De'Andrey

Lucille Ball

Monkey Business

In 2002, a young man called the rescue ranch to set up an appointment for him and his wife to come out and possibly adopt one of our "Utopian Dogs." He wanted to know if it would be okay for them to bring along their pets to make sure that they would get along. I told him that it would be fine for them to bring along their dogs. I was then told that they weren't dogs.

Figuring that it must be cats, I told him that it would be fine to bring the cats out; wrong again. This guy informs me that they weren't cats. Puzzled as to what kind of pets these people had, I asked him to tell me what kind of pets they had. His answer was monkeys—six, to be exact.

A week later, the "monkey people" arrived on time to check out our dogs. Tony and I really liked them from the get-go, and their little monkeys were absolutely precious. All of them were dressed in little cowboy and cowgirl outfits!

During our walking tour, Tony and I were told by this nice, friendly couple that they lived near Galveston in a big house, which they shared with their six monkeys, including their bedroom. Near the end of our walking tour, Tony and I were told that they also had annual monkey slumber parties, where six or more of their monkey-loving friends would come over to their house and bring their monkeys, so that all of the monkeys could play together. They told us that their parties were a lot of fun, and that we should consider coming to one.

Unable to resist, I asked, "Is it BYOM?"

"Yes," they answered, "and BYOB."

With our walkabout completed, it was now time for the monkey people to tell us which dogs they were interested in, so we could try them out with their monkeys. As the little monkeys threw their cowboy hats at each other, the couple told us that they had narrowed it down to Flash Gordon, Monica Lewinsky, and Wonder Woman.

After attaching leashes to their monkeys and putting little blue jean jackets on them, we went to see Flash Gordon, a sweet, one-year-old black Labrador Retriever. Well, that didn't work out at all. When the monkeys first met Flash, they immediately began hitting him really hard on the top of his head, which made Flash mad. Needless to say, we were out of there in a flash.

Now it was Monica Lewinsky's turn. She was a large, tan mutt. Unfortunately, having witnessed what the monkeys had done to her friend, Flash, next door, she refused to come near the little posse, and growled. Strike two!

We were now batting zero with two fouls against the monkeys. With fingers crossed, we headed over to Wonder Woman's pen. Wonder Woman was a small yellow Lab mix, who was as sweet as she could be, and she shared her pen with Mickey Rooney, one of our favorite gigantic mutts.

When we arrived at Mickey's and Wonder Woman's pen, Mickey took off running with his tail between his legs the minute he saw the cowmonkeys. Wonder Woman did just the opposite. With their monkeys perched on top of their heads and riding side-saddle on their shoulders, the couple was approached by Wonder Woman slowly, wagging her tail. Within a matter of minutes, the miniature wranglers were calmly sitting on Wonder Woman's back and behaving nicely, with Wonder Woman seeming to enjoy them. After about an hour of hanging out with Wonder Woman in the OK pen, the couple decided to adopt her.

I went to the trailer, called Kinky with the good news, and then prepared the adoption papers for Wonder Woman. As soon as the couple had signed the paperwork, Kinky arrived at the rescue ranch so he could meet the monkey people and their adorable monkeys, and to also say good-bye to Wonder Woman.

After the introductions, the woman placed two of the monkeys on top of Kinky's head. Kinky tried to remain calm and act nonchalant as their little monkeys began nit-picking Kinky's hair. Then they scooted down to Kinky's shoulders, and, as one jumped on Kinky's back, pretending to ride him like a cowboy as he clutched Kinky's neck tightly, the other monkey sat unruffled on his shoulder and began primping Kinky's sideburns and kissing his ear.

Max Swafford, who had come out to work with our dogs that morning, made the comment, "Well, we now have proof that Kinky definitely has a monkey on his back. Ride 'em cowboy!"—which caused all of us to burst out laughing. The only one not laughing, of course, was the Kinkster, who was growing more uncomfortable by the moment. He knew that he had to cowboy up or monkey up, so he lit up his cigar. That did it! The monkeys flew to their owners' arms, and the rodeo was over.

Later that day, after the monkey people and their monkeys had left the rescue ranch with Wonder Woman, I told Kinky about how nice the young couple had been by sharing their monkey stories with us, and also about them having annual monkey parties.

Kinky asked me what I thought they did at the monkey parties, and I replied, "I guess they watch *Planet of the Apes* movies. Who knows?"

Kinky chuckled. Then he asked me to get in touch with the monkey people to ask if we could come to one of their monkey parties. He said, "Tell them I'm a big fan of Charlton Heston, and I love their monkeys, and to give Wonder Woman a hug from me."

To B&B or Not to B&B?

Before the sun came up on Friday morning, August 3, 2003, Ben and Tony had gone out to the barn to saddle up our two wild mustangs to go for an early morning ride around Echo Hill Ranch. When they returned to the rescue ranch, I had some exciting news for them. Don and his wife, Gerri Dickerson, who own Mountain View Cabins in Medina, had called the rescue ranch to tell us that their pet wild pig, Chops, whom they had rescued months earlier, was ready to be picked up and taken to the rescue ranch.

A month or so earlier, the Dickersons had come over to the rescue ranch to meet Kinky and all of us. During their visit they told us about their latest rescue—a baby wild hog! They had found an orphaned, weak, little male wild piglet wandering around and had taken him home to nurse him back to health.

Their little pig was raised with their two sweet, large Golden Retrievers, Monty and Chloe, and, to the Dickerson's surprise, this little wild piglet seemed to act more like a dog than a pig. As the weeks passed by, this little fella began growing and growing and growing, until he was nearly the size of their dogs. Chops had also learned to fetch and play ball, too—and his favorite thing of all was to be petted. It was like he was a dog in a pig's suit.

After unsaddling the horses and turning them out, Tony and Ben drove over to the Dickerson's to pick up Chops and bring him to the rescue ranch to live with our other domesticated rescued pigs.

While Tony and Ben were gone, I decided to change Chops's name to Harley Davidson, because he was a real hog. When they arrived back at the rescue ranch with Harley riding between them on the front seat, I was sick that I didn't have my camera with me.

Ben and Tony carried Harley into the pig pen and set him down right in the middle of the other pigs to see if our pigs would accept him or try to kill him. To everyone's relief, our pigs didn't seem to care one way or another about Harley being there, even though he looked so different from the rest of them. For one thing, Harley was reddish-orange colored and covered with big, round black spots, and he had a snout on him that was as long as a football field. He was absolutely adorable.

Kinky came over just after Harley arrived and fell in love with him. Harley let him pet him, throw the giant ball for him, and gently took treats from his hand.

Harley soon became the most popular animal at the rescue ranch. Everybody fell in love with him and wanted to play with him. Visitors would take pictures of him playing with their children—who would always beg their parents to please let them adopt him—and he would delight everyone with his ball-fetching antics. Harley was definitely a clown and a great entertainer.

In two months' time, Harley had doubled in size, but he was still as sweet and playful as ever. One morning, Tony went outside to feed the animals and discovered that Harley was a "chicken murderer!" He had killed two of Tony's favorite pet hens; this was not good news.

Tony and I spent the entire morning and early afternoon trying to decide if we should build a special pen for Harley or remove the chickens and our rooster, Alfred Hitchcock, to a new chicken coop. Fortunately, we didn't have to do either—our problem was solved for us later that afternoon.

A very nice couple from Vanderpool, Texas, Tom and Rhonda Fousek, who own A Peace of Heaven, a bed-and-breakfast, cabins, and RV Park, came out to the rescue ranch to take a tour. During the tour, Rhonda, a licensed therapist who does family, marriage, and individual counseling, asked me if she could bring some children she was working with out to the rescue ranch to interact with our animals, as part of their therapy work. Of course, the answer was yes, knowing that it would be as beneficial to the children as it would be for our animals.

At the end of the tour, Rhonda and Tom met our pigs. As soon as I called Harley's name, he came running up to the fence to be petted. Rhonda and Tom fell in love with him immediately.

"I love Harley!" Rhonda said. "Is he this good with everybody?"

"Yes," I answered, "but he's not real good with chickens."

After a brief visit in my writing studio, Tom asked me if I could show him a certain dog, so we excused ourselves and went back to the dog pens. As soon as we were far enough from my studio so that Rhonda couldn't hear us, Tom told me that the real reason that he had asked me outside was to ask me if he could adopt Harley as a surprise anniversary gift for Rhonda. He told me that he needed to build a pig pen first and asked if Tony and Ben could possibly help him.

Knowing that we needed to get Harley moved as soon as possible, so he wouldn't kill any more innocent chickens, my answer was yes! On the way back to my studio, Tom and I made a secret plan about Harley and the fence building.

As soon as Tom and Rhonda had left the ranch, I told Tony about Tom and our little secret plan. He liked Tom and Rhonda and was all for it. When I phoned Kinky to tell him the good news that Harley was getting adopted, he was sad at first, but happy that Harley was going to such a good home, where he would remain a celebrity at Tom and Rhonda's "Peace of Heaven."

In a matter of days, Tony, Ben, and Tom had Harley's pen built. On November 12, 2003, Tom drove out to the rescue ranch to pick up Harley.

As soon as Tom arrived, Kinky came over to the rescue ranch to meet Tom and to tell Harley good-bye. After meeting Tom, Kinky went over to Tom's truck to see if Harley was going to be okay and to bid him farewell. To Kinky's surprise, Harley seemed totally fine in his temporary cage and didn't appear to be bothered at all about leaving the rescue ranch, making it a lot easier for Kinky to say good-bye to him.

As Tom drove away with Harley riding comfortably in the back of his pickup, Kinky said, "Harley is one great pig—I'm going to miss him. And, Nance, keep in touch with Tom and Rhonda and make sure they know that we want him back if it doesn't work out."

Knock on wood, it has worked out. And every time that Rhonda comes out here to work with a child, she tells me that Harley is doing great, and everyone who stays at A Peace of Heaven spoils him with treats and attention.

Rodney, the Red-Nosed Rain Deer

On December 2, 2004, early in the evening, Tony was outside feeding the dogs. A cold front was on its way; the temperature outside was dropping steadily, and it was starting to rain lightly.

I was inside my trailer vacuuming up the day's collection of dog and cat hair, when my dogs, who were out in the front yard, began barking something fierce. I figured that someone must have pulled up and that was why they were barking, so I turned off the vacuum cleaner, called my dogs inside, and then went out to the porch to see who was out there.

Nobody was out there. I looked around the yard and over by the gate stood a giant buck. As I stared at the buck and he stared back at me, I said, "Hi there, deer."

The deer cocked his head and continued to stare at me. I knew this was a Kodak moment, so I ran inside the trailer, grabbed my Sony digital camera, and went back outside. I figured I needed to capture a picture of him so everyone would believe me when I told them about him. I carefully walked down the steps and said, "Here, deer."

The deer didn't say anything but began slowly walking the fence line towards me. I started shooting pictures one after another, until he was staring at me eye-to-eye at the gate. I didn't know what to do; I looked to see if I could see Tony out by the pens, but he was out of sight.

I then slowly reached over the gate and patted this deer on the top of his head. The deer seemed to like it, so I keep patting him and talking to him. In the back of my mind, I'm thinking: this is unbelievable! I'm a deer whisperer and didn't even know it!

I was so full of myself about being a deer whisperer, I decided to take things a little bit further. I slowly unlatched the gate and stepped outside of the yard. The deer took a couple of steps backward, to give me room, and then gently nuzzled my shoulder. I was on cloud nine, and it had stopped raining.

As I whispered to him, I petted the deer on his neck, chest, hip, and head. This went on for about ten minutes; he and I were buddies.

When I heard the sound of Kermit, our green four-wheeler, I knew that Tony was finished feeding and was heading back to the trailer. When Tony was in sight I slowly waved my arms, cautioning him to slow down so he wouldn't scare the buck away. Tony pulled up slowly and parked about twenty feet from where the deer and I were standing.

"Can you believe this?" I said. "I'm a deer whisperer! I can't wait to tell Kinky!"

Tony seemed unimpressed and said, "Step slowly back into the front yard. That deer is dangerous."

I don't usually mind Tony, or anyone else for that matter, but I heeded his advice. I stepped back inside the yard and latched the gate.

"Tony, he is not mean. Please come pet him. I don't think he's dangerous at all," I said.

Tony reached into the back of the pickup and slowly pulled out a cardboard box that was approximately six feet long and ten inches wide. It was the box that our new weed-eater had come in. He held it up vertically, close to his body, like it was a shield, and then he began taking these little, baby side steps moving slowly past the deer towards me. Every time that he scooted, I wanted to laugh out loud. I thought, how in the world could Tony think that a weed eater box could protect him from an attack deer?

Well, I hate to admit it, but the weed eater box did protect him, and Tony made it safely inside the front yard unharmed. The whole time that this was going on the attack deer did nothing, thank goodness; he just stood there watching Tony boot-scoot himself into the front yard.

I started laughing once Tony was inside the yard and had latched the gate. Then I asked him why he thought the deer would hurt us.

"Nance, that's a young buck, and when they hit puberty they become very mean. Don't you ever go up to a buck again. You're lucky he didn't try to kill you or tear you up!"

"Okay, okay. But what are we going to do with him?" I asked.

"I'll bet you he is one of Robert and Sherry's pet deer," Tony said. "I'm gonna go call them now." Tony went inside the trailer.

Robert and Sherry live on the big ranch next door to us, and, from time to time, Sherry rescues orphaned fawns and raises them, and then releases them back into the wild when they are ready to make it on their own. In fact, Sherry and her family have taken every baby deer that has been brought to us.

We have only had about ten baby fawns brought to us since we started the rescue ranch. The majority of the fawns have all come from tourists spending time down here in the Hill Country. When the tourists see a baby fawn standing alone, they assume that it is lost, so they grab it. Little do they know that the mother deer is standing no farther away than a hundred feet, grazing.

Tony came out of the trailer. "It's theirs," Tony said. "His name is Rodney. They're on their way over here right now."

"I can't wait to tell them about what happened!" I said.

"You're not going to tell them about the weed eater box, are you?"

"Yes, Tony," I said. "That's the funniest part. Buck up!"

When we heard Sherry's truck, Rodney cocked his head in its direction and then turned around to look for them. When Sherry and her children arrived to pick Rodney up, Rodney ran over to them to greet them. After I told my story to them, they unlatched the tailgate and told Rodney to load up. I was in shock. I had never heard of a deer loading up in the back of a truck.

"Are you telling me that Rodney will load up in the back of the truck?" I asked.

"Sure," Sherry said. "Our dog taught him. He'll ride all day long, all over the ranch, in Robert's truck. He loves it."

Rodney decided that he didn't want to load up in Sherry's truck, so her daughters walked him home instead.

That evening, I told Kinky all about Rodney's visit and the weed eater box, and showed him pictures. Kinky enjoyed looking at my pictures and asked me if Rodney ever came over again to please call him, because he would like to meet the deer.

A few weeks later, Ben Welch and Will Wallace, who were doing some Echo Hill Ranch landscaping over by the dump, came over to the rescue ranch to tell us that they had just met Rodney and asked us if we would call Robert and Sherry. They told us that they had heard a dog bark in the brush near them, and, when they went to check it out, they found Rodney and a Red Heeler dog. They told us the dog and Rodney seemed to be friends; when Ben called Rodney's name, the deer and the dog went to Ben and Will to be petted.

Before Tony went to the trailer to call our neighbors, Ben teasingly said to Tony, "Can we borrow your weed eater box? We might need it, and we promise to bring it right back."

Everyone, including Tony, broke out laughing. Tony told him no, and then went to the trailer to make the call. When Tony stepped out of the trailer onto the front porch, he said, "The dog's name is Red. Sherry is on her way over here right now."

Ben and Will drove off in their pickup to go meet Sherry over by the dump, in case she needed their help.

Later that day, Will and Ben told us that Sherry had told them that she and Robert had been given a little Red Heeler pup, and it had grown up playing with Rodney. She told Ben and Will that the two of

THE ROAD TO UTOPIA

them go everywhere together, and Red is the one who taught Rodney how to load up into the back of their truck.

On December 18, 2005, Tony and I were getting dressed up to ride with Kinky to Kerrville to see Billy Joe Shaver perform. We had planned this in advance and would be meeting up with our friends Max Swafford and Jon and Sandy Wolfmueller around seven o'clock, before the show.

About forty-five minutes before we were supposed to leave the ranch for Kerrville, Kinky called.

"Tony, Nancy?" Kinky said, to the answering machine. "Pick up the phone! I think Rodney's here!"

Tony picked up the phone, said a few words to Kinky, hung up, called Robert and Sherry, and then took off for Kinky's Lodge.

When Tony arrived at the Lodge, Kinky was outside hand-feeding Rodney Cheerios. Tony advised Kinky to stop feeding Rodney because Rodney would be showing up every day over there and might get hurt by his dogs if Kinky were not home. That fell on deaf ears, and Kinky continued to feed Rodney and pet him. Sherry showed up a few minutes later, visited with Tony and Kinky, and then loaded Rodney up into the back of the pickup and drove him home. The entire time that it took the three of us to drive to Kerrville, we talked about Rodney.

We met up with our friends at seven o'clock and enjoyed one of the best shows that any of us had ever seen Billy Joe Shaver perform. It was a magical night!

Rodney has not visited us lately, but we look forward to it when he does. Sherry told us that Rodney and Red are doing fine and to ask Kinky to please not feed Rodney anymore Cheerios, so he will stay put on their ranch.

Jeepers Creepers

At 12:30 p.m., on Monday, May 5, 2003, the rescue ranch had a horse emergency!

Tony and I had just finished eating our lunch out on the porch, when a big, white Chevy truck came speeding up to our trailer. At first we didn't know who it was, but by the time it stopped in front of us we knew who it was. Sherry Selement, our good friend and neighbor, jumped out of the pickup, and, with a panicked expression on her face, quickly told us there was a horse with its two back hooves stuck in the Echo Hill cattle guard. Sherry jumped back into her truck and took off like a bat out of hell, with Tony and me right behind her in our truck.

When we arrived at the cattle guard, Robert, Sherry's husband, and Nelda Cabiness, good friend and the wrangler for Echo Hill Ranch, were struggling with a downed, frightened horse, trying to keep it from breaking its legs. When we got out of the truck, Tony told me not to get near the dangerous horse, and then he and Sherry took over Nelda's and Robert's job, so Robert and Nelda could try to get the horse's hooves out of the steel guard.

Watching the struggling horse trying desperately to stand up, and knowing full well that if it were to get up, its legs would snap and the horse would most likely have to be destroyed, and all that I could do was say prayers.

After about ten minutes, Robert and Nelda, using a long, heavy steel pipe, got one of the horse's hooves freed! Unfortunately, though, the horse thrashed so hard trying to get up that it threw Sherry backwards about ten feet, where she landed hard against a fence post. With the wind knocked out of her, Sherry, after a few seconds, finally smiled and told us that she was okay, and then she slowly stood up, rubbing her back.

Feeling helpless standing there watching the four of them bravely risking their lives for this horse, I had an idea! Looking into the back of the pickup, I found exactly what I was looking for—grease. I grabbed the little can of chain saw grease, went to the cattle guard, and poured it on the remaining hoof stuck in the iron trap, hoping that it might help them slide the hoof out.

Right after I had done this, with Tony and Sherry lying on top of the horse to keep it down, it thrashed hard again, and this time it was Tony's turn to be knocked off. He landed almost in the same spot Sherry had landed, but he wasn't as lucky as Sherry had been. He told us that he thought his leg was broken, and I could tell that he was in a lot of pain.

Before Tony could make it back over to help Sherry, Robert and Nelda freed the hoof. With that, Sherry hopped off the horse, and it jumped up—standing on all fours.

Thinking quickly, before the horse could take off, Nelda slipped a halter over its head, so they could inspect it first. Besides the horse being near exhaustion, nothing was broken—but maybe Tony's leg. Because the horse had a little limp, Nelda decided to put it in the corral so that she could observe it for a few days. We followed Nelda, in our trucks, as she slowly walked the horse all of the way back to the corral.

By the time we had reached the corral, Tony's lower leg had swollen to twice its size, and he was definitely hurt; I also had found out that the horse's name was Jeepers. After Nelda had fed, watered, and doctored the horse's legs, we left and went our separate ways.

When Tony and I returned to the rescue ranch, he was unable to show me his leg, because he couldn't pull his jeans off—they were too tight. We had to use scissors to cut off his pants so we could check out his injury.

I nearly fainted when I saw Tony's leg. It wasn't blue—it was black! I didn't know what to do, so I called Kinky.

Kinky immediately ordered me to take him to the emergency room in Kerrville, but this was not the advice I wanted to hear. I told him I would, but didn't.

My thinking was, if Tony could walk on it, it wasn't broken, and, besides that, we didn't have insurance, and we could not afford the expense of the emergency room. Finally, we decided to drive to a near-by town that had a clinic. Before heading out, Tony called Ray Bruinsma, one of our great part-time workers, to ask him to please come over to the rescue ranch to feed the animals while we were gone. We passed Ray, headed for the rescue ranch, before we even got off our two-and-a-half mile dirt road.

The clinic I chose was a bad choice, unfortunately. We had to wait over an hour in the waiting room, and, since it was near closing time, the doctor told us that his X-ray machine was broken, and had the nurses clean and wrap Tony's leg and then told us to go to the emergency room in Kerrville to see if it were broken; that cost us over a hundred dollars. That was money well spent.

When we arrived back at the rescue ranch, Ray was still feeding the dogs outside. Once we reached our trailer, Tony grabbed a feed bucket and went to feed our miniature horse, Trigger, Jr., in our backyard. I went inside the trailer to find that Kinky had left a message on the answering machine to call him.

While I was on the phone to Kinky, telling him about the clinic, with him demanding that we go to the emergency room immediately, Tony nearly pooped in his pants in the backyard.

After promising Kinky that we were headed for the emergency room in Kerrville, Tony walked into the trailer looking exactly like Frankenstein. He was white as a sheet, dragging his bad leg and coming towards me like he had seen a ghost! He would have been a dead ringer for Mr. Frankenstein if he had had screws coming out of his neck.

Before I could flee, Tony told me that on his way to feed Trigger, Jr., he had literally just crossed paths with a six-foot-long rattlesnake! He told me that halfway to Trigger, Jr.'s, feed bucket, as he took a step, he had actually stepped over the snake as it was headed in another direction. He told me that the snake had gone under our trailer.

Being terrified of snakes, that was all that I needed to hear. I would never venture outside again.

While Tony was still in the restroom, I had a lightbulb moment. I called one of our veterinarians to ask if it would be possible to X-ray Tony's leg, because we didn't have health insurance and it would be a whole lot cheaper than going to the emergency room. The vet told me no, and was sorry.

Two minutes passed when our phone rang; I checked our Caller ID, and it was the same veterinarian calling. I picked up the phone, and the veterinarian told me to bring Tony in for an X-ray. When Tony came out of the restroom, I told him that one of "our vets" had agreed to do the X-ray. Because I was so exhausted, Tony asked Ray to drive him to the vet's office, and Ray agreed to do it. Off they went.

An hour later, Tony called me from the "secret location" to tell me that his leg was not broken, and he and Ray were headed back to the rescue ranch. With that good news, I phoned Kinky. He was very happy to hear that Tony's leg was not broken, and then I told him about one of our veterinarians doing the X-ray, and saving us a ton of money.

Even though we were not in the same room, I could tell that Kinky was beside himself, and speechless. Finally, he started laughing. I then explained to him that many of my friends go to their veterinarians for X-rays, because it is so much cheaper, and they even take their kids to see them.

When Tony and Ray returned home, they told me that our veterinarian had made them promise, and for me to promise, to never reveal his or her name. And the good news was the X-ray was free—no charge!

The next day, we passed Sherry on the road, headed to town. We flagged her down and asked her about her back. She told us that it was pretty sore, but she thought that she would be fine, she hoped.

Before we took off, we told her to call our vet to get it checked out—and that it wouldn't cost her a thing!

It took over six months for Tony's leg to finally return to a lighter shade of pale, and Jeepers finally recovered, and we still don't know where the snake is.

Oh, Crappy Day

On December 6, 2004, I received a phone call from a woman at the local TV station in Kerrville, Texas. She was calling to invite me, and a dog of my choice, to come on her afternoon show to promote our rescue ranch and to discuss animal issues. I told her that I would get back to her.

I went over to Kinky's to get his input, because he had been on her show several times. When I told him about the invitation he encouraged me to do it. So, I came back home and called the woman. After checking our calendars, we set the date for December 22, 2004, at 12:30 p.m.

During the next two weeks I found myself getting nervous about doing the show. I felt that Kinky would be better doing the show than me because he was used to being interviewed, and people would enjoy it more seeing him on TV than me. Nearing my debut date, I shared my concerns with Kinky about doing the show. His response was that I was full of you-know-what, and he told me to quit worrying and do it. He promised me that I would enjoy it and that it would be fun. So, I heeded his advice and quit worrying, sorta.

The day before the show, I went from pen to pen to pick out who my TV partner would be. Tony and Kinky had already recommended that I use one of our twelve new puppies, all from the same litter—so I ended up picking Sponge Bob.

Sponge Bob, like his litter mates, was a Libra. He was born on September 26, 2004, and was one of the twelve puppies born that day, in a six-hour period, from a dog that we had rescued. Sponge Bob looked like an oversized black Labrador puppy, and could have passed for one, but we knew he wasn't because his mother was a gigantic Mastiff/Catahoula mix. Also, Sponge Bob was the biggest in his litter— he weighed twenty-nine pounds and wasn't even three months old!

On December 22nd, at 8:30 in the morning on a cold, rainy day, Tony brought Sponge Bob to the trailer so we could give him a bath. He was so big that he didn't fit in the kitchen sink, so Tony gave him a bath in the bathtub. Sponge Bob didn't like getting a bath. He gave Tony a hard time by jumping out of the tub several times and running through our trailer slinging water everywhere. We used all of the towels that we had by the time we had finished drying him off.

Now it was time to blow-dry Sponge Bob. After cleaning off our kitchen table, Tony lifted him up and sat him on it. Sponge Bob did not care for this, either. When I plugged in the hair dryer and turned it on nothing happened; the hair dryer was dead. I felt this was an omen—a bad one. Tony thought I was full of you-know-what.

In a mild panic, I called Kinky in New York City to ask if he had a hair dryer that we could borrow. He was in the middle of a live interview and couldn't believe his ears that I had called him in New York City to borrow a hair dryer. After explaining to him why I needed the hair dryer, and that I had hoped to get one from the Lodge, not from

New York City, he told me that he didn't have one here or there. So, we laughingly blew each other off and hung up.

As the clock was ticking away the minutes, Sponge Bob's coat was as damp as a wrung-out washcloth. With all of our towels soaking wet, Tony used up two rolls of paper towels to finish drying Sponge Bob. I thank God that we had Scott paper towels, because they did the trick. While Tony worked on Sponge Bob, I cleaned up and dressed for the TV show.

Picking out what I was going to wear was fairly easy for me since I am not much of a dresser. I came out of our bedroom wearing a white, long-sleeved, buttoned-down oxford shirt with my pastel pink overalls, hot pink cap, and white tennis shoes. I had even put on a little eye make-up and added a beaded turquoise necklace to finish off my look.

Before taking off for Kerrville, which is twenty-two miles away, Tony fed Sponge Bob, and he cleaned his plate. Then it was time to dress Sponge Bob: he wore a red bandana tied around his neck. It was now time to go. I had given myself an extra thirty minutes just in case something happened, and thank God that I did.

Rain was pouring down as Tony loaded Sponge Bob into a crate in the back of the Explorer, along with some chew toys and an old quilt. We were dressed to kill—lookout Kerrville, here we come!

I said good-bye to Tony, started the engine, and we were on our way. By the time we reached Highway 16 I switched on the radio, and Buffalo Springfield was singing "something's happenin' here," while Sponge Bob was singing his own tune in the back of the car. We were only about eight miles from the rescue ranch when the song ended on the radio.

As soon as it had ended, a horrible smell filled the entire vehicle. I immediately recognized the smell—Sponge Bob had pooped in his crate. I wanted to pull off the road, but there was no place for me to safely stop. So, the next thing I did was roll down the windows, but the heavy rain forced me to roll them back up and make another plan.

By the time that we arrived in Kerrville, I headed straight to the pet store. As soon as I had parked the car, I ran inside and told the store owner about Sponge Bob pooping and us fixin' to be on a TV show. The kind owner handed me a roll of paper towels.

There I was out there in the parking lot with Sponge Bob on a leash, covered in poop, trying to clean him. The rain helped some, but not enough, so I did the best that I could under the circumstances. I removed the quilt from Sponge Bob's cage, rolled it up, and put it in a plastic bag to take back to the house. With him as clean as he was going to get, I loaded him back into the crate and closed the door.

I went back inside the pet store, thanked the owner for helping me, and then purchased some doggie cologne that was pretty expensive. Time was of the essence, so I quickly squirted Sponge Bob so that he now smelled like a spring forest, or at least that is what it said on the spray can. We were now running late, so we took off headed for the television studio.

When we arrived at the station, we had only three minutes before we were to go on the air. K. D., the woman who was going to do the interview, was outside waiting for us in the parking lot, and she had an umbrella. As I lifted Sponge Bob from the car, my back made a horrible sound and had just gone out on me. I guess that is why in show business they say "break a leg," so nothing worse happens to you. As I tried to wipe the remaining poop off of Sponge Bob, I told the woman what had happened. I then re-squirted him with cologne, and we followed the woman into the station wet and laughing.

She quickly introduced me to the staff as we rushed past them to get to the set. As soon as we arrived she rapidly positioned Sponge Bob and me on a love seat opposite her chair.

"Lights, camera, action," the producer of the show said. "We're live."

The lights came on and the cameras started rolling. The lights had scared Sponge Bob, so he started crawling over to me and plopped himself into my lap, as K. D. was introducing us, and he smelled to high heaven; his scent was now a mixture of wet dog, perfume, and poop, all combined. I would have called it "Eau de Toilet!"

As the interview went on, my back was killing me, my legs had gone to sleep, and so had Sponge Bob, but I kept smiling and answering questions that the lady threw at me. In no time at all, the show was over and Sponge Bob had slept through the entire show.

When the lights went out, K. D. thanked me for being on the show. I apologized up and down to her and the staff for running late, and for Sponge Bob smelling up the place, but she just laughed and told me not to worry—the show had been fine.

As my TV partner and I got up from the couch, I looked down to find my baby pink coveralls covered in poop, and it was also all over my white shirt! I was so embarrassed to think that I had been sitting there on that couch, looking like I had come from a mud wrestling match. I told K. D. after loading up Sponge Bob, "At least the audience thought it was mud and couldn't smell us."

Sponge Bob and I arrived back at the rescue ranch thirty minutes later. Tony rushed outside to greet us and said, "You were great on the show! I recorded it! But, how'd you get all of that mud on you?"

"Don't ask," I said, "You wouldn't believe me if I told you."

On February 9, 2005, Sponge Bob (Diaper Pants) was adopted by some friends of Kinky's and now lives happily up in Austin, Texas. His new family absolutely adores him, and the latest report we have received is that Sponge Bob is so gigantic that he can rest his head on the kitchen table while sitting down!

Karma

Tony and I almost got ourselves arrested in August 2005, on the account of three raccoons.

He and I were returning home to the rescue ranch from a short trip to West Texas, when we pulled into a service station to fill up the truck just outside the city limits sign of a small town. Even though it was in the middle of the afternoon, the small service station appeared to be closed, because there were no cars in sight, but we decided to give it a try anyway.

After stopping, I went to the front door of the service station and it opened—they were open. When I walked inside, I immediately felt the bad vibes of the place, and was about to turn around and walk out, when a woman hollered over from the deli area.

"You need something?" she asked, in a rude manner.

"Yes," I said. "We need to get some gas."

"I'll be there in a minute," she growled.

Then a woman exited the indoor restroom looking like ten miles of bad road, with her hair all ratted up, a cigarette hanging from her lips, and sporting a black eye.

"I'll take care of her," the worn-out woman said, as she slammed the restroom door behind her and slowly began walking towards me.

"What you need?" she asked as she went behind the counter.

"Gas," I answered.

"We don't take credit cards," she said. "You got cash?"

"Yes, I do."

"Put a twenty on the counter, and I'll turn on the pumps," she said, sourly.

I pulled out a twenty and handed it to her, and then she flipped a switch. Not wanting to hang out in there, I went outside to talk to Tony.

I told him about the two creepy women inside, as he pumped the fuel. When I was finished telling him about them, he said, "Go tell those women that there are three raccoons trapped inside their empty dumpster, trying to get out. The temperature is over a hundred, and they are burning up in there and have no water and nothing to stand on but that hot metal. They look nearly dead. Listen, you can hear them trying to claw out."

I listened to the poor raccoons and felt sick. I rushed back inside the service station and told the two women that were now sitting on stools behind the cash register about the trapped coons, and they laughed at me.

"If they are stupid enough to get in there—then it's their fault," the ignorant redneck woman stated. "We got more coons around here—just leave them be—good riddance."

"Would it be okay if we let them out?" I asked.

"Sweetie, you touch that dumpster," she snapped back, "and I'll call the police. That dumpster is private property."

I was so mad at her that I wanted to slap her. I could not believe how cruel and cold-hearted she was towards animals. I marched back outside to tell Tony, and he told me to go back inside and distract them. He would take care of it, even though the ugly dumpster had "no trespassing" and "private property" signs decorating its sides.

I reluctantly went back inside the service station. As the two stupid, trashy women sat on their stools staring at me, with their backs to the front window, I started a dumb conversation with them about where to find a good restaurant nearby.

My asking them for their opinion seemed to empower these two you-know-whats; as they began arguing back and forth about which hole-in-the-wall cafe was better, I pretended to listen to these wackos and watched Tony walk over to their private-property dumpster, lift a handle, and open the side door to free the three hot, near-death, dehydrated hostage raccoons!

After the three coons had made their escape, Tony closed the dumpster door and gave me a thumbs up before returning to the truck to finish gassing up. When he turned off the gas pump, I was wearing the biggest grin that I have ever worn. I then quickly paid the wannabe ladies for the fuel and triumphantly walked away from their bad vibes.

The last time I drove through that small town, there was a big, hand-painted "Out of Business" sign hanging from the service station.

Thank God and Greyhounds

This is a true story that actually happened at the rescue ranch—but didn't. The people who I only use first names for have been changed to protect them, their organizations, and the rescue ranch, but the ones with both a first and last name, such as Richard Pryor, for example, are the true names of the real people that were involved in this unbelievable rescue attempt.

In the late afternoon of August 29, 2005, Kinky, Tony, and I had an emergency three-way telephone meeting to discuss Hurricane Katrina, and what we could do to help the abandoned and suffering animals down in Louisiana. Even though our meeting was brief, the bottom line was that we had to get involved now! Time was of the essence. We made a plan.

I put Plan A into action immediately following our conversation. I called the Red Cross in San Antonio, Texas. When I reached the Red Cross, after trying to explain that the rescue ranch was at their service to take in at least twenty-five dogs, I was passed from one coordinator to another at least four times. Finally, a man named Bill answered his phone, and, after my explaining to him what our ranch was offering, he took my name, the rescue ranch's name, our phone number, fax number, and e-mail address and promised to get back to me soon.

Well, for Kinky, Tony, and me, soon wasn't good enough. So, I called several other animal organizations to try to enlist our ranch to help them, but to no avail; they all said, "We'll get back to you." Frustrated by the nonchalance shown by these well-known animal welfare agencies, and after tearfully watching a sad, but beautiful, Bloodhound floating down the Mississippi on a rooftop, all alone, I broke down and cried for hours, as I am sure everyone did that saw that news footage.

The following morning, feeling depressed because no one had called for our help, Tony and I drove to the Kerrville pound and rescued four dogs which were on death row. Before delivering them to Hoegemeyer Animal Clinic, we named the two male Dachshunds Brooks and Dunn, and the two medium-sized sister mutts June Hartley and Ellen Degeneres.

When Tony and I returned to the rescue ranch, the only message on our answering machine was from Kinky wanting to know how our rescue efforts were going. I telephoned him to tell him about us rescuing the four from the Kerrville pound, but that there was still no word from the organizations we had contacted, even though now they were begging for money on the TV, and the newscasters were now telling everyone to donate to them, while flashing their phone numbers. We were disgusted about the bureaucratic bologna and frustrated about what was not being done to help the Katrina animals.

The only phone call the rescue ranch received that Tuesday was from Dr. Craig Janssen, from Hoegemeyer Animal Clinic, to inform us that he had spayed and neutered all four of our dogs, but Dunn and Ellen had heartworms and he was starting treatment on them in the morning.

Wednesday morning, August 31, 2005, Richard Pryor's wife, Jennifer Lee Pryor, called the rescue ranch crying and left a desperate message on the answering machine.

Her last words were, "Today is my birthday, and it is the saddest birthday in my life, because no one is doing anything to help the animals down in New Orleans and Mississippi. Richard and I are sick and our hearts are breaking. Nancy, please call me as soon as you get this."

That morning at 10:30, I phoned Jennifer. I listened as she tearily told me about an emergency rescue situation in Louisiana that she and Richard hoped our rescue ranch could help with. She told me that she had been contacted about sixteen Greyhounds in New Orleans that were stuck up in an attic with no food or water, needing desperately to be rescued, and the owner of the Greyhounds was up in the attic with them, and the woman was now unreachable by phone!

After reassuring Jennifer that we would help rescue the sixteen Greyhounds, she gave the phone numbers of the contact people, Elvira and Ashley. Before hanging up, Jennifer told me that she and Richard were sending a check to pay for the rescue mission.

As soon as that conversation ended, I phoned Elvira and introduced myself. She told me that she was in Louisiana and would rescue the dogs, when she got the okay, and for me to call Ashley, who was coordinating the rescues. Before calling Ashley, I took two extra baby aspirins, so I wouldn't have a heart attack.

Ashley and I talked for over ten minutes, working out a plan as to where we would be hooking up with Elvira to pick up the dogs to bring to our rescue ranch. It was decided that their truck would meet us in Temple, Texas, on Saturday afternoon, but there was still no definite time set—just the afternoon.

After that phone call, I immediately began calling some of our best friends and ranch volunteers to ask if they could help us pick up the dogs in Temple on Saturday. Ben Welch, Will Wallace, Jim Cravotta, Max Swafford, and Paul Emerson stepped up to the plate and said yes! The wheels were set in motion.

After lining this out with our volunteers, I phoned Kinky to tell him about the Greyhound rescue mission. Kinky was delighted to hear that our rescue ranch was finally going to rescue some dogs from Louisiana. Then he told me that he had just rescued an old friend from New

Orleans, Reverend Goat Carson, who had lost everything. Kinky told me that Goat would be coming to Echo Hill Ranch soon and would be staying as long as he wanted.

The rest of the day was spent communicating back and forth with our volunteers, lining up crates and trailers, and making plans on getting the dogs. It was exhausting for all of us, but, by the end of the day, everything was worked out. Or so we thought.

At five minutes past six o'clock, Jennifer called crying. She told me the Army would not let Elvira get the dogs because a levee broke. With this news we were now on hold. After that phone call, I began calling all of our volunteers to update them on our rescue.

On Thursday, September 1, the phone would not quit ringing. Our volunteers were anxious for updates, but I had none, because Elvira and Ashley had not returned my phone calls. To say the least, it was a nail-biting morning. Finally, in the afternoon, Ashley called with an update—we were still on hold, but there were hundreds of thousands of dogs and cats that needed to be rescued, too. She told me that Elvira was overwhelmed with the disaster but was certain she would be able to get to the Greyhounds. I was then told that it wasn't sixteen Greyhounds, it was now thirteen. I didn't ask her why the number had dropped from sixteen to thirteen because I knew that I would not be able to handle it.

I then phoned our volunteers to update them. In between the calls that I made, I found myself saying little prayers for the dogs in the attic and found out that everyone that was involved with our Greyhound rescue was doing the exact same thing.

Friday morning, September 2nd, I called the Kerrville pound, Paul Emerson, Dr. Lloyd Leifeste Veterinary Hospital, and Hoegemeyer Animal Clinic to ask if we could borrow their large dog crates, because we had only four large cages. Everyone's response was the same: "Come and get them!"

Bless Paul, he told me that he would deliver his two large crates to the rescue ranch before noon, and Jim Cravotta called to tell me that he had lined out a horse trailer that he could borrow from his friend. We were set!

Ten minutes after Paul arrived to deliver his two crates, our good friend and dedicated volunteer Will Wallace, from Austin, showed up at the rescue ranch pulling a long trailer. Paul left quickly, knowing that we needed to go pick up the loaned dog crates in Kerrville. After Paul left I went inside the trailer to find the answering machine flashing urgently at me. Ben Stroud, our good friend from Dallas, had just called and made an offer that the rescue ranch couldn't refuse. He had gotten wind of our Greyhound rescue mission and had called to tell us that he already had four friends lined up in Dallas to meet Elvira in Shreveport, which was much closer for her. This was truly a godsend.

I called Ben Stroud immediately. After a short conversation, Ben told me it was the least that they could do to help the Greyhounds. He went on to tell me that friends of his were offering the use of their homes to foster the dogs until he would be able to deliver them to us. He also had lined out a couple of veterinarians ready and willing to treat the dogs for whatever was needed, but he still needed our crates.

I put Will on the phone with Ben Stroud to make a plan for getting the crates up to him. After a brief conversation, Will hung up and called Ben Welch in Austin to see if he could help deliver the crates to Stroud. Ben told him he would do whatever it took to help the rescue ranch. After that conversation Will called Stroud and they worked out a plan to meet up in Waco on Saturday morning.

When I got the phone back from Will, I called Jim Cravotta, Max Swafford, and Paul Emerson to thank them for their efforts, and to let them know that Ben Stroud would be picking up our dogs; the only thing that they needed to do was to enjoy their Labor Day Weekend. With all of that said and done, Will and Tony took off for Kerrville to gather the borrowed crates.

As soon as they were gone, I phoned Jennifer to give her an update. Next, I phoned Elvira. She told me to make sure that Ben Stroud had sixteen IV kits, vitamin B injections, and Sub-Q fluids when they arrived in Shreveport to pick up the dogs. I then called Leifeste Veterinary Hospital office to see if they had kits, shots, and fluids. They did, and Dr. Leifeste's wife, Betty, told me they would be ready to be picked up around 5:30.

At 2:31 that afternoon, Susie McQuade called the rescue ranch to tell me that they found out about our Greyhound rescue from a friend of Ben Stroud's, and that she had just gotten off the phone with Ben. Susie explained to me that she and her husband, John McQuade, were members of the Greyhound Adoption League in Dallas, and her husband was the Chairman of the Board. This group had an air-conditioned "hauler," and these angels from Dallas were offering their services to go and rescue the Greyhounds for us. Susie told me that Ben Stroud thought it sounded great and hoped that we would accept their offer.

I was so excited hearing her proposal I accepted it immediately. Everything was coming together! I told her about the need for the shots, IV kits, and fluids, and Susie told me not to worry because they had it covered. I promised Susie and John that I would call them the minute that I heard from Elvira or Ashley.

After that exciting conversation, I took a few more baby aspirins. Then it hit me—I needed to call Tony and Will to cancel the crates! Unfortunately, Tony had forgotten to take our cell phone, and Will's was turned off. So, I did the next best thing: I called the pound and the clinics and told them not to give the crates to Will and Tony, and to please ask them to call me. Fortunately, Tony and Will got the message, called the rescue ranch, and headed home crateless. Next I called Leifeste Veterinary Hospital and canceled the medications that I had ordered. After I had done that, the waiting game began.

Around six o'clock, I received a call from Ashley. She called to give me the home phone number of the woman that was in the attic with the Greyhounds. Her name was Leticia. As soon as I hung up, I dialed Leticia's number. A man answered the phone, and I pretty much scared the heck out of him. When he answered, I told him who I was, and that I was from the Utopia Animal Rescue Ranch, and we were fixin' to rescue his Greyhounds. Our conversation went something like this:

"What?" the man asked. "I'm Leticia's husband. Leticia is at the grocery store. You want to do what?"

"A woman named Elvira," I explained, "told us that y'all had sixteen Greyhounds that urgently needed to be rescued. She told us that y'all had flooded, and Leticia and the sixteen Greyhounds had been up in the attic with no food or water for days."

"What?" he asked again. "Ma'am, my wife and I rescue Greyhounds, and we have ten of them—they are our pets. We don't want you to come and take our dogs."

"Well, who is in the attic?" I asked.

"Nobody, that I know of," he replied.

"So, the Greyhounds are okay?" I asked, feeling really stupid.

"Yes, they are fine," he answered. "We never flooded or lost electricity. We're fine."

"Well, I apologize for the misinformation that was given to me," I said. "I'm glad you and your wife and the Greyhounds are safe. I'm sorry for bothering you. Good-bye and take care."

I then called Jennifer to tell her about the Greyhounds; she was glad the Greyhounds were fine but sick that FEMA and the bureaucrats were so unorganized and not letting the rescue groups in.

Before I could call Susie and John, Kinky's younger sister, Marcie, called to let me know that she and Reverend Goat Carson had arrived safely at Echo Hill, and that she had been saying prayers for the poor Greyhounds in the attic. She told me Goat was anxious to meet Tony and me and was so excited about our rescue ranch's Katrina involvement that he had called all of his friends from New Orleans, including Aaron Neville of the Neville Brothers and Dr. John, to tell them, "Kinky and the rescue ranch are bringing in twenty-four Greyhounds from New Orleans!"

I told her that her prayers had been answered, and the Greyhounds were fine, because they had never been in danger in the first place; it was all miscommunications. I was relieved that the Greyhounds were fine, but thinking about all of the time and energy that had been wasted had me so upset that I was scared that I was going to literally have a heart attack.

God bless Tony, because he brought me a few more baby aspirins to swallow, and a tall glass of wine to wash them down. It worked, too, because I slept like a log that night.

The first thing I did Saturday morning was to call Susie to tell her the Greyhounds were fine and never in danger. I thanked her and John and their wonderful organization for being there for us. I told her that Ashley had told us not to give up because Elvira had told her that there were still thousands of dogs and cats needing to be rescued and the government still wouldn't let the rescuers in.

When Susie heard this, she offered to help, again. She told me the Greyhound Adoption League of Texas would help us rescue mutts or whatever. They still wanted to help the poor animals in Louisiana. With that kind gesture, I gave her Elvira's phone number, and Susie suggested that the three of us have a three-way conference call later in the day.

At one o'clock sharp, Susie, Elvira, and I were connected. Elvira told us that there were hundreds and hundreds of dogs and cats needing rescuing, and, near the end of our meeting, we decided that Elvira would contact Susie to set the time and date. Then Susie would call me just to keep us posted.

Around 4:30 that afternoon, Susie called to tell me that she thought everything was running smoothly, and she figured that we would be getting our dogs delivered to us Sunday evening around six o'clock. Later that evening, Tony and I, after much discussion, decided that we would take eleven of our rescued dogs to Kerrville in the morning, so we could free up several pens to make sure that we had ample space for our rescued Katrina dogs.

Sunday morning, Marcie joined us for breakfast and we had an enjoyable visit until it was time for Tony and me to take some of our dogs to Kerrville—knowing full well that we were going to have to make two round trips to get all of our dogs to Leifeste Veterinary Hospital and Hoegemeyer Animal Clinic.

I drove the pickup on the first run, with Kris Kristofferson, Molly Ivins, and Blackie riding inside the cab licking my face the entire trip. Tony followed me in the Explorer with Chase Manhattan, Loretta Lynn, and Tammy Wynette. We delivered them to the Leifeste Veterinary Hospital.

When we pulled up, Dr. Lloyd Leifeste was waiting for us outside his hospital. He helped Tony unload the dogs and take them to the kennels. Before leaving, Dr. Leifeste told us that he would do anything to help us with the Katrina dogs that would be coming in.

On round two, I drove the Explorer with Bridgette Bardot and Tappy on board. Tony followed me in the pickup with Roxanne, Rufus, and Jack Kennedy, and we deposited them safely at Hoegemeyer Animal Clinic. A little after eleven o'clock, before we returned from Kerrville, John McQuade left a message on our machine that Elvira was running late, because she had been under a curfew, and asked that we call him.

As soon as I walked in the door, I phoned John. He told me that Elvira had appeared to be a little bit shaky on the phone, and still had no idea as to when they were to meet up. He told me that some very good friends of theirs, Jeff and Chris, who were with an animal rescue group that was already down in Baton Rouge, had offered to hook up with Elvira and bring the dogs to us. John recommended that we use them, because his group of volunteers had to return to their day jobs on Monday. We had run out of time, and he apologized.

There was no need for him to apologize after all of the effort that they had given towards this rescue effort. I returned his apology, and thanked him and asked him to thank his organization.

Before calling Jeff and Chris, I decided to call Elvira to let her know that Chris and Jeff, from another rescue group, would be hooking up with her, and to let her know they were already in Baton Rouge waiting for her. Elvira sounded confident, so I called Jeff and Chris, and introduced myself to them, and thanked them for offering to help us. Then I gave them Elvira's cell number. Around eight o'clock that evening, Ashley called to tell me that they had talked to Chris and Jeff, and they would be hooking up with them early in the morning in Baton Rouge.

Monday morning, many friends called wanting news about the arrival of the dogs and asked if they could come out. My answer to all of them was a polite "thanks for wanting to help, but we have it covered," explaining that too many people would stress out the Katrina dogs even more.

Two of our favorite, hardworking part-time workers from the Medina Children's Home, Daniel Hudson and De'Andrey Wingwood, showed up promptly at nine o'clock in the morning to help Tony clean pens and feed the dogs. Tony had asked them to help him out, because they knew our dogs and were great handling them.

At 12:15, I called Chris and Jeff to see if they had gotten our dogs. Chris told me that they had finally met up with Elvira, and he did not have anything nice to say about her. He said that she had shown up with only two puppies—and that was it! She had no other dogs. He also told me that she had cussed some men out who were also waiting on her to pick up dogs. In Chris's own words, "Elvira was a flake and there was chaos everywhere and no one seemed to be organized."

Chris told me that he and Jeff were on the road and now headed home to Dallas, and apologized about not bringing us any dogs. He was very frustrated. Once again, I apologized to them for wasting their time and thanked them for their efforts. I told him that the only one who should be apologizing now was me.

Jennifer was the next to be called. I told her that I had just talked to Chris and Jeff, and, as far as the rescue ranch was concerned, we were pulling off of Elvira and Ashley. I told her everything that Chris had told me, and she asked me for their phone number. Jennifer also told me before hanging up that Elvira had called her an hour earlier asking her to send several hundred dollars, because they had run out of cages. Putting two and two together, it didn't take a rocket scientist to realize that things were an absolute mess.

I then went outside to tell the guys about the failed rescue, and they were disappointed, to say the least. After the dogs were fed and the pens cleaned, Tony sent De'Andrey and Daniel back to the Medina Children's Home to enjoy what was left of the holiday.

Tony and I spent the day resting, until Harley Belew called to tell us that he had just rescued a dog from under his house that was in bad shape. Tony asked Harley to bring the dog out to us. Harley and his family arrived at the rescue ranch in under twenty minutes with the young male dog.

When we first saw the poor, blood-soaked dog, he managed to wag his tail at us. I was amazed that he would wag his tail at us when a human had done this to him. Tony knew instantly what had happened to this young mixed-breed dog. He told us that some creep had shot the dog at close range using a shotgun!

Tony took off to call Dr. Leifeste about the dog. When he returned to us, he told us that Dr. Leifeste told him to get the dog to him immediately. As everyone departed the rescue ranch, I told Harley that I had just named the little dog Harley in honor of him for helping the dog. Harley and his family liked that.

Dr. Leifeste was waiting for us outside when we arrived at his hospital. Tony carried the bloody little dog inside the clinic and put him on the examining table. Tony's diagnosis had been correct—it was a shotgun wound. Even though the little dog was in a lot of pain, Harley had the spirit to live and even tried to wag his tail as Dr. Leifeste examined him on the table. One of Harley's ears had been nearly blown off, but Dr. Leifeste told us that he thought he could save it. The poor little fella also had numerous holes in his body, which Dr. Leifeste examined closely.

Before we left the hospital, Dr. Leifeste told us that he felt the little guy would survive, but he needed surgery immediately. Tony and I then left the hospital, so as not to be in Dr. Leifeste's way. We arrived back at the rescue ranch around 8:30 that night and went to bed early.

Tuesday morning was spent hauling our rescued dogs back from Kerrville, and they seemed happy to be back home. By noon, the rescue ranch was almost back to a state of normalcy. A couple of days later, we received a sizeable donation from Jennifer and Richard thanking us for all that we do.

On Friday, September 16, we were finally able to rescue some Katrina dogs from some rescue groups in Kerrville. At the time we had room for four dogs but ended up taking six. Before we arrived at Dr. Jonathan Brooke's River Hills Animal Clinic to drop off Marcia Ball and Boudin, because they needed to be treated for heartworms, we had named the other four dogs Dr. John, Gumbo, Tulane, and Tabasco.

Marcia Ball and Dr. John were adopted within the first week to super homes. On Monday, October 3rd, we brought in four more Katrina victims, Napoleon Dynamite and his sister, Belle, Stella, and Jazz, and we plan to get more in the near future.

Not to forget Goat, Kinky's personal evacuee: he is doing fine at Echo Hill Ranch, giving lectures at Schreiner University and getting his life back together. Oh, the reason why Rev. Goat had been so enthusiastic about the Greyhounds was, he later told Kinky, "I thought you meant buses."

As for Harley, he stayed at Leifeste Animal Hospital for over a month-and-a-half, had to undergo several surgeries on his ear, and is now doing fine and loves everyone that he meets at the rescue ranch. When Betty Leifeste presented us with Harley's bill, I almost fainted. Instead of being over a thousand dollars, as it should have been, she and her husband only charged us two hundred dollars! And, every time that we have gone back to Leifeste Animal Hospital since then, the first thing Lloyd or Betty asks is, "How is Harley doing?"

Today, October 17, 2005, my fifty-fourth birthday, as I finish writing this book, no one from the Red Cross or the FEMA-endorsed organizations has called, faxed, or e-mailed us back. We are still planning on rescuing some Louisiana dogs, but, like I explained to Kinky, we can't ignore the dogs at the Kerrville pound; they deserve to be rescued, too.

After reading this story, many readers may ask if what we do is worth it. Kinky's, Tony's, and my answer to that question is, "Hell, yes!" We love what we're doing, and we feel that we are fortunate to be able to do it, thanks to everyone who has helped us.

To Be Continued (knock on wood!) . . .

Money, Money, Money

One morning, a few months back, while I was doing the "Steve & Harley Show," they asked me if I was going to give a portion of my profits from the sales of this book to the Utopia Animal Rescue Ranch. Of course I was; I had planned on doing that from the very beginning but was dumbstruck when they asked me on air and I didn't know what to say.

After the radio show was over, I called my older brother, Ron Culbertson, up in Dripping Springs, Texas, for his advice. I told him that I was thinking of giving at least half of my profits to the rescue ranch and asked him what he thought.

He paused for a couple of seconds and then began laughing. When he finally quit laughing he said, "Nance, you can't be a philanthropist until you have money. Right?"

We then both broke out laughing. He was absolutely right.

"Don't worry about it now," he said, "it's too early. Wait and see how your book does and then decide."

The Three Muttsketeers & Daisy

Muchas Gracias

After having written over eight pages listing the names of everyone who has helped support our rescue ranch, I realized that if I accidentally left out just one person's name or misspelled it—it would be hurtful and undoable to correct, so I deleted all of the names. Besides, y'all know who you are and so do we, and Kinky, Tony, and I thank you and send you our best! And please remember, none of this could have ever happened without your support and we know it!

For anyone wishing to support and become a part of the Utopia Animal Rescue Ranch we welcome you! As always, we need money, volunteers, adoptions, and foster homes. If you are interested in helping, please check us out at **utopiarescue.com** or contact us at:

Utopia Animal Rescue Ranch
966 Echo Hill Road
Medina, Texas 78055
or
Phone: 830-589-7544
Fax: 830-589-7545

P.S. I just have one final thing to say,
"I love you, Tony, Kinky, and Ben!"

Epilogue for Cuddles

On January 4, 1993, the cat in this book and the books that preceded it was put to sleep in Kerrville, Texas, by Dr. W. H. Hoegemeyer and myself. Cuddles was fourteen years old, a respectable age. She was as close to me as any human being I have ever known.

Cuddles and I spent many years together, both in New York, where I first found her as a little kitten on the street in Chinatown, and later on the ranch in Texas. She was always with me, on the table, on the bed, by the fireplace, beside the typewriter, on top of my suitcase when I returned from a trip.

I dug Cuddles' grave with a silver spade, in the little garden by the stream behind the old green trailer where both of us lived in the summertime. Her burial shroud was my old New York sweatshirt and in the grave with her is a can of tuna and a cigar.

A few days ago I received a sympathy note from Bill Hoegemeyer, the veterinarian. It opened with a verse by Irving Townsend: "We who choose to surround ourselves with lives even more temporary than our own live within a fragile circle . . ."

Now, as I write this, on a gray winter day by the fireside, I can almost feel her light tread, moving from my head and my heart down through my fingertips to the keys of the typewriter. People may surprise you with unexpected kindness. Dogs have a depth of loyalty that often we seem unworthy of. But the love of a cat is a blessing, a privilege in this world.

They say when you die and go to heaven all the dogs and cats you've ever had in your life come running to meet you.

Until that day, rest in peace, Cuddles.

Kinky Friedman, *Elvis, Jesus, & Coca-Cola*

Utopia…